MW00465133

Edgar Cayce's
Egyptian
Energy Healing

Edgar Cayce's
Egyptian
Energy Healing

Shelley Kaehr, PhD

A.R.E. Press   •   Virginia Beach   •   Virginia

Copyright © 2019
by Shelley Kaehr, PhD
2nd Printing, October 2019
Printed in the U.S.A.

All rights reserved. No part of this book may be reproduced or trans-
mitted in any form or by any means, electronic or mechanical, including
photocopying, recording, or by any information storage and retrieval
system, without permission in writing from the publisher.

A.R.E. Press
215 67th Street
Virginia Beach, VA 23451-2061

ISBN-13: 978-0-87604-945-7

All biblical quotes come from the King James Version of the Bible.

Healing Symbol Illustrations by Shelley Kaehr

Edgar Cayce Readings © 1971, 1993-2007
by the Edgar Cayce Foundation.
All rights reserved.

Cover design by Christine Fulcher

Dedication

I dedicate this work to future generations in the hope that this material can aid you on your path to oneness with the infinite.

Contents

Acknowledgments

Special thanks and gratitude to the incomparable Cassie McQuagge for championing this project from the beginning. Huge thanks to Kevin Todeschi, John Van Auken and Jennie Taylor for their support of my work through the years. Special thanks to my awesome editor, Stephanie Pope, and the entire team at A.R.E. including Allison Parker Hedrick, Kristie Holmes, Zaire McCullough, Christine Fulcher, and Cathy Merchand. I owe a debt of gratitude to my family, friends, and the many students and clients who continue to inspire me through the years. I thank you all!

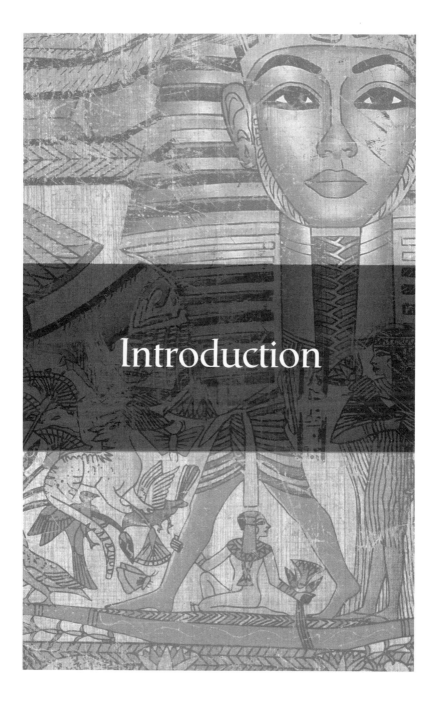

Introduction

GC: You will have before you the healing group gathered here in this room. Because of our desire to carry on Thy Work in accordance with Thy Will, we seek at this time a clearer understanding of the healing forces and their interaction through us as members of this group. Please explain to us that which we need at this time in carrying forward this work.

EC: Yes, we have the group here, as a whole, as individuals. In seeking to be a channel of blessing to others through such a group, well that individually all self-condemnation be laid aside, that self be wholly free in that source of power as would bring hope, faith, confidence, and HEALING to those who seek through this channel to be made more aware of His love in their lives. Not in arrogance by any one; rather seek through meditation, singleness of purpose, to be guided in that channel in which each may BE a channel of blessing to those who seek. 281-3

Shockingly, for nearly twenty years now, I have been professionally training students in energy–healing methods. My personal journey into the world of energy healing began after I returned from a trip to Egypt, Turkey, and Greece back in July of 2000. Shortly after I returned home, I went through a near–death experience.

When I traveled into the light, I came back with knowledge about things I did not consciously understand, such as how to move energy and shift frequencies. To catch my conscious mind up with what was happening, I went to school. Lots of school. I became a Reiki Master, took courses in any modality I could get my hands on, and made those teachings my own.

During those years, I became fascinated by the work of the world's greatest psychic, Edgar Cayce, and was fortunate enough to write two books about Cayce's use of gemstones—information I find fascinating and important to this day.

Incredibly, even though Cayce gave his readings years ago, the wisdom he and Source brought through in the life readings continue to inspire and assist people around the world—physically, materially, mentally, emotionally, and spiritually.

The deeper I dive into the Cayce readings, the more I find, and the more I am compelled to keep seeking. When I read passages such as the one at the beginning of this chapter where a group gathered together to discuss how to keep this movement and the knowledge of Edgar Cayce alive, I am inspired to do my part to ensure that this work continues to help people for generations to come.

That's exactly what happened as I underwent a journey of several years to compile this book. Inspired by invaluable information from the life readings, I discovered so much Cayce left us in terms of how to do healings and how to approach different concepts. Along the way, I even found the tools to create a healing technique I hope will be of benefit to those who are guided to come along on the journey of healing and self-discovery.

I am a big believer in taking information and breaking it down so it can be applied to our daily lives in order to assist in enhancing our journey in body, mind, and spirit. That's exactly what we're going to do here; guided by Cayce's wisdom, we will explore what was said and interpret how we can apply this to our daily healing practices.

It is my hope that by the end of this book, you will be able to take Cayce's instructions and follow them yourself to enhance your frequencies and bring a sense of increased balance to your life. Let's get started!

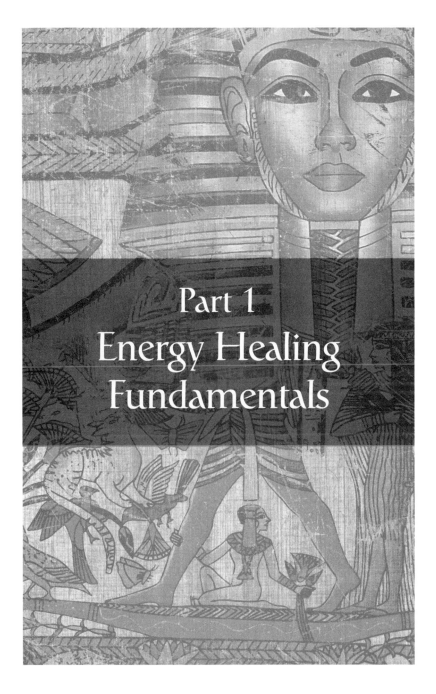

Part 1
Energy Healing
Fundamentals

We're going to explore an exciting new technique through the Edgar Cayce life readings, but before we do, I want to include a section on some fundamentals that every healing practitioner needs to know. For those of you who are new to the world of energy and spiritual healing, this will give you an overview to guide you through this journey. But I also believe that it's always good to go back to review the basics occasionally to keep the mind fresh and to set the tone for any work to be more effective. So, if you're already an experienced healer, this section will provide a short review.

Know that wherever you are on your path, it's perfect!

What Is Energy Work?

Know this; that all healing of every nature must come from a mental attitude created by either that activity within the system as food, as medicine, as activities, the principle of which is constructive in aiding those deficient portions to become coordinant with the rest of the system for constructive forces.   1436-1

Energy work is the conscious process of shifting the non-physical energy that exists within your physical shell to such a degree that you begin to attract what you truly want in life—be it better health, more abundance and stability, or great love and peace. We are all made of energy, and when we're experiencing dis-ease, it means that we must shift that energy into a new form in order to release what we do not want and begin to create what we do want.

I absolutely love the reading at the beginning of this section because Source explains this idea so well. When your energy is off, it might take a variety of things to get back on track—be it food, medicine, vitamins, and activities such as exercise or dance. We are going to explore many of these things as the book goes along. The bottom line is balance. We must somehow work to achieve balance in not only our physical body but also in the unseen forces within.

Energy work is a massage for the soul, consciously moving energy around to bring the body into a state of wellness and our minds and spirits into a place of peace. Cayce mentioned the importance of aligning the soul with the physical body in many life readings, including the following:

> For only the soul lives on. That which had a beginning has an end. Thy soul is a part of the beginning and the end, and thus is one with the Creative Forces or God—if ye will so act in thy relationships with thy purposes, thy desires, as to make that body (with which the soul is clothed) as companionable with Him.
>
> 1641-1

Once we tune in to our soul, a shift takes place, and the soul experiences a knowing that transcends all knowing. By changing frequencies, you automatically begin to attract what you want by aligning yourself with a new energy.

I write a lot about how we can use gems and stones to aid in this shift, but in reality, you can use the focused attention of the mind to do the same thing, and that, my friends, is what energy healing is all about.

In any form of healing, the goal is to change the current frequency to one that is more balanced and in rapport with peace and optimal results. Sounds simple enough. And yet, working with our consciousness to overcome our life lessons and challenges to achieve lasting happiness and peace throughout our lives is actually a lifelong endeavor. As human beings, we are a continual work in progress. We might be balanced and peaceful one day, only to have things shift and change the next. Life is a constant flux of movement, and so working on our energy is a journey, not a destination. It's part of what we incarnate in earth to learn.

The key to understanding energy healing is the idea that you are not your physical body. You are so much more than that, and to achieve optimal health, happiness, and peace in your life, you must acknowledge the unseen aspects of yourself. In other words, as Cayce said himself, it's all about vibrations.

Vibrations

Remember, there is the ability also within self to raise the vibrations . . .   1861-10

Everything in the universe is made up of vibrations—cells and atoms vibrating at varying rates to create different physical expressions in the outer world. To shift reality, we simply change our vibrations to rise above what no longer serves us and begin to get into what I call energetic rapport with the unseen vibrations of that which is for our highest and best.

The Cayce readings are filled with detailed information about vibrations and how we can achieve balance by aligning ourselves with certain frequencies. I've discussed this at length in my other two Cayce books on gemstones.

In this study, I want to look more at the vibrations themselves and how we can take the invisible force that exists everywhere around us and shift our vibrations, so our external reality is more in alignment with peace, joy, and happiness. Cayce's past-life readings offered specific directions for how recipients could enhance their vibrations to ensure they would enjoy their full potential in the current life.

There is literally no telling what you are capable of when you raise your frequency so that your energy is running at full capacity. You have unlimited potential.

Auras and Colors

. . . each individual was and is as yet clothed with ITS individual color—as ye call aura.   1436-2

The Edgar Cayce readings are filled with discussions about the importance of recognizing and working with the aura—the colored energy field that exists around the physical body of each person. Colors change over time depending on health and mood, and this color can tell us much about people in terms of how they are feeling and what they might do to improve their overall well-being in body, mind, and spirit.

One way you can tell about how a person is feeling or what energetic blockages might need to be worked on is by studying the aura of the person, and then go from there. How? Source gives an excellent explanation in the following:

> . . . In the body the tone is given off rather in the higher vibration, or the color.
> Hence this is a condition that exists with each physical body . . .
>
> 440-6

Throughout his lifetime, Edgar Cayce had the amazing ability to see people's auras. Depending on what he saw, Cayce recommended remedies and treatments for people to strengthen these fields. Let's take a brief look at a few of the recommendations Cayce and Source made based on colors he saw in people's auras.

Red

> At least two to three times each week—three times in the beginning—for twenty to thirty minutes we would use the Infra-Red light over the knee area.   1207-2

> (Q) Who would you recommend to give the Infra-Red treatments?
> (A) Anyone that has an Infra-Red machine!   1207-2

Years ago, I was guided to use the color red on one of my healing books on stones. Some people loved it, and others . . . well, let's just say they weren't exactly fans. Red is a strong color, a grounding energy, and for some, it's a little too much to take. That said, as you can see in the reading above, Source did recommend red in the form of the Infra-Red light to people for healing.

In the following, he suggested a more subdued color:

Never the drab, never too much of the red-red, but those of the more delicate hues—but decided in hue.   1401-1

I started working with red years ago because of the grounding properties so I could hopefully become more focused, and I believe it helped. It's all about balance.

Yellow

(Q) To what colors do I vibrate . . . ?
(A) . . . the entity will respond to certain shades of yellow . . .
478-1

Yellow is another color that often has mixed reviews. I've become a fan of yellow after learning that it positively impacts health and well-being, according to Feng Shui practitioners. Also, the citrine stone I write about in my gem books vibrates to the yellow ray which assists with creating material abundance and strength.

Green

. . . But in most instances where there is needed a change in vibration, the projection of a green light is preferable—because green is the healing vibration . . .   3370-1

Cayce could not be more on the mark with this statement. Green is indeed the healing color and brings physical healing to the person and a nurturing sense of calm to any situation.

Again, I can mostly cite this from my work with stones. All green stones help people heal vibrationally.

Blue

Blue is the love influence . . .   1401-1

Blue is a peaceful energy that surely calms our emotions, and I would suppose that for some it could indeed bring the energies of love. Blue also aids communication and eases emotional stress.

Purple

(Q) What is her aura?
(A) Purple . . . purple the spiritual development.   1401-1

For years I was absolutely hooked on the color purple. It sends us into the ether, out into the unified field where we can leave the troubles of the material world behind, and as Cayce describes, it is definitely the color for spiritual development.

Purple can leave you a little ungrounded, which can be a good thing at times, depending on the situation.

Violet

(Q) To what color or colors does my body vibrate best?
(A) To violet . . .   303-2

Keep these up; and keep those applications that are made at periods—as indicated—of the ultra-violet ray light, for STIM-ULATING the circulation.   1901-2

Edgar Cayce often recommended the use of the ultraviolet light to assist people in healing. Violet combines the purple and red energies together to combust into a powerful healing force that can truly shift your energy in the right direction.

To shift the aura colors within the physical body, you can either meditate on the particular color you are trying to enhance, or you could simply play the note that resonates with the color. The easiest way to do this would be to play all the notes, beginning from C to C, envisioning the colors as you go, and set your intention to achieve balance within all energy centers of the body.

This brief overview is by no means the totality of information on this interesting aspect of the life readings. For more details on auras, I highly recommend the amazing book *Edgar Cayce on Auras & Colors*, written by aura experts A.R.E. Executive Director Kevin Todeschi and Carol Ann Liaros who go into great detail about all the ways Cayce worked with auras. I saw Carol Ann's workshop on auras when we both spoke at the A.R.E. Annual Psychic Development Conference in 2018, and I can tell you there's a lot to learn here. It is all incredibly interesting if you are so inclined.

Music

As is known, the body in action—or a live body—emanates from same the vibrations to which it as a body is vibrating, both physical and spiritual. Just as there is an aura when a string of a musical instrument is vibrated—the tone is produced by the vibration.   440-6

What an amazing description Source provides to describe how the body attunes itself to the proper note.

Vibrations translate to musical notes on the scale and colors in the rainbow spectrum. When you're off, simply attune yourself, or retune yourself to the proper notes and soon you will achieve balance in the body.

Source was actually able to tell people what notes they resonate best with, as in the following reading:

Q) To what colors do I vibrate, and what note of the musical scale?
(A) Just off note, as it might be said, in the music. Hence C and combinations between—not OFF note, but C and its combinations.   478-1

How I wish Cayce were here now to let us know what would work best! Then again, can't you feel within yourself what makes you happiest or feel best at any given moment? When it comes to music, I know I can by simply listening to the kind of music I'm in the mood to hear at the moment. At times, I might listen to upbeat jazz; other times I enjoy brooding classical music. I've recently enjoyed taking hip–hop

and Zumba classes with a ton of salsa and méringue music built in to
the routines.

Music and dancing were a huge part of the ritual of shifting frequencies during Cayce's time in Egypt. We will explore this more later in the
book, but for now, know that music is healing, it is helpful, so follow
your intuition to find the tune that's best for you.

In healing, our bodies are best aligned when they are attuned to the
notes on the musical scale. For vibrational shifts to occur, the frequencies around and within the body will shift until they achieve the state
of perfection represented by music.

Likewise, those musical notes also correlate with colors on the rainbow spectrum that are found within the body—the chakras, which we'll
look at next.

NOTE	COLOR	CHAKRA
C to D	Red	Root
D to E	Orange	Sacral
E to F	Yellow	Solar Plexus
F to G	Green	Heart
G to A	Blue	Throat
A to B	Indigo	Third Eye
B to C	Violet	Crown

The Seven Chakras

(Q) How may I bring into activity my pineal and pituitary
glands, as well as the Kundalini and other chakras, that I may
attain to higher mental and spiritual powers? Are there exercises
for this purpose, and if there are, please give them.
(A) As indicated, first so FILL the mind with the ideal that
it may vibrate throughout the whole of the MENTAL being!
Then, close the desires of the fleshly self to conditions about
same. MEDITATE upon "THY WILL WITH ME." Feel
same. Fill ALL the centers of the body, from the lowest to the
highest, with that ideal; opening the centers by surrounding self

first with that consciousness, "NOT MY WILL BUT THINE, O LORD, BE DONE IN AND THROUGH ME." And then, have that desire, that purpose, not of attaining without HIS direction, but WITH His direction—who is the Maker, the Giver of life and light; as it is indeed in Him that we live and move and have our being.   1861-4

The chakras (originally spelled *cakra* which is Sanskrit for *wheel* or *circle*) were first mentioned in the Vedas, the oldest texts of ancient Hinduism, written sometime between 1700-1100 BCE, and were referred to as wheels of light.

While Cayce and Source never actually mentioned the word *chakra* directly, Source did provide information on how to balance these important energy centers by focusing on their ideal state of being. For chakras, these ideals are represented by the same exact frequencies of colors.

When these wheels of light are fully open and properly functioning within our bodies, they vibrate at the same speed as different colors of light. If we were actually able to see the chakras, they would look like colored tornadoes, beginning at the base of the spine and working up to the top of the head. One of the main objectives in any kind of healing work is to enliven these energy centers within us because their openness is directly related to our physical and mental well-being.

Let's examine how each of our chakra centers function.

First Chakra: Root
Color: Red
Gemstones: Ruby, Hematite
Musical Note: C

Then keep close to the earth; that is, where the feet may oft be on the ground itself, for the earth—ground—is the mother of the material, but spiritualize all by every ideal, every idea, every plan being purposeful; but for all and not for self to have its way alone.   3479-2

The root, or first, chakra is located at the base of the spine and vibrates to the color red. When functioning properly, this chakra keeps us grounded in earthly activities and helps us feel centered and connected to the earth. If we are feeling "spaced out," confused, or disconnected from reality, there may be a blockage there. In Eastern thought, the root is the location of the Kundalini energy that resides at the base of the spine and eventually leads us to enlightenment. It is also one of the chakra centers that assists our ability to manifest on the physical plane.

Grounding is an incredibly important aspect of physical life and our purpose. We face challenges and difficulties in our lives that cause us to want to escape reality and float around in other realms. The technological advancement of our society has done much to assist mankind, but one of the downsides is that people are in a continual trance while working with their technology, and as such, are not as grounded as they need to be. Grounding and being here to experience the life we signed up for in our current incarnation are among the lessons of the root chakra.

Second Chakra: Sacral
Color: Orange
Gemstones: Carnelian, Red Jasper
Musical Note: D

> . . . one becomes attuned to everything in nature; yet nature
> IS a manifestation of every form that we may see of the divine,
> making force manifest of the Creative Energy . . .   451-1

The sacral, or second, chakra vibrates to the orange color frequency and is located just below the navel. As the seat of creation, this important energy center is the part of you that is able to create and manifest. Combined with the root chakra, these are the primary sources for our creative energies.

The second chakra is also our sexual center. The healthy functioning of the first and second chakras combined enables us not only to create, but to actually finish things and bring them out on the physical plane. An example of someone with a well-functioning second chakra is an artist who produces a painting and takes it to an art show to sell, or a business person who creates an idea and takes that idea out into the world, putting it to practical use.

Third Chakra: Solar Plexus
Color: Yellow
Gemstones: Citrine, Yellow Sapphire
Musical Note: E

. . . having the courage to carry out that ideal—makes the difference between the constructive and creative forces or relationships
and those that make one become rather as a drifter or a ne'er-do-
well, or one very unstable and unhappy.   1401-1

The third chakra, or solar plexus, is located at the convergence of the
rib cage. It vibrates to the color yellow and is the seat of our personal
power. How we stand up for ourselves and demonstrate courage are the
lessons of the solar plexus chakra. Our solar plexus area is also about
material wealth and the creation of abundance. Blockages here may
hinder our ability to create money in our lives. Additionally, fearless-
ness, courage, and willpower are all aspects of our solar plexus chakra.

Fourth Chakra: Heart
Color: Green
Gemstones: Emerald, Rose Quartz
Musical Note: F

As is said, in the heart love finds its way.   281-51

The fourth chakra is the heart. It surprises many people that the heart
chakra vibrates to the color green, since we often associate it with rosy
red or pink. While these colors are also very healing to our hearts, it is
actually the healing green of Mother Nature herself that best resonates
with our heart center. Since heart disease is still a major challenge in
the United States and around the world, heart-chakra issues involve
humanity's ability to hopefully be successful at shifting our attention
to loving each other, embracing diversity and oneness as a collective
whole, while ridding ourselves and our world of hatred, bigotry, and
greedy materialism. Lessons of the heart deal not only with loving

others, but with loving ourselves, which can be even more challenging for many people.

Fifth Chakra: Throat
Color: Blue
Gemstones: Sapphire, Sodalite, Blue Topaz
Musical Note: G

. . . A good speaker, but speak truth—ever . . .   3155-1

The fifth, or throat, chakra is light blue and is all about communication. By "communication," I mean how we speak our truth in the world. Are we speaking up, or are we shoving our true opinions down in the spirit of political correctness? This is a huge issue these days. We are living in a supposedly free society, and yet speaking out can be stressful and even dangerous in some cases. Still, we must prevail, and as we are able to accept ourselves more and share our ideas as well as the personal truth as we see it, we open our throat chakras.

Have you ever noticed either in yourself or others when you have a little tickle in your throat? Or you may notice someone coughing and you know for a fact that person is not ill? I see this quite often. A lot of times this means the person disagrees with what's being said and is trying hard to suppress the desire to speak up.

If you notice yourself doing this from time to time, as I am sure we all do, you likely need to say something difficult to someone. This is a tough lesson for all of us, potentially because so many of us have suffered persecution in past lives as a result of our beliefs. Conscious effort to open this center can really pay off in the long run because the tension from not expressing our truth can eventually become quite a burden on the body, not to mention the long–term difficulties in society, in general, when we are unable to say what we need to get to our truth.

Sixth Chakra: Third Eye
Color: Indigo
Gemstones: Amethyst, Iolite
Musical Note: A

(Q) How can the body develop her psychic ability?

(A) In the quietude of self's study of the experiences through the
earth's plane, these will be opened . . .   2708-1

The sixth chakra, located in the center of the forehead, is known as
the third eye. This is our mystical, psychic, intuitive center, and it is the
one chakra many of us would most like to open. Most of the people I
meet who are on the spiritual path are looking for ways to open their
third eye in the hopes of gaining insights to make life flow with greater
ease. This is an ability we can all develop with practice, as Cayce mentioned many times in the readings.

The third-eye chakra vibrates to the color of indigo, a purplish blue.
Many times, in spiritual work, you may see a purple light inside your
head. This happens quite a bit with my hypnosis clients. Sometimes
what they are experiencing is the opening of their intuitive centers,
since much of the hypnotic work is done using their own intuition.
Pay attention next time you notice a purple light. It could be a sign
you are opening up!

Seventh Chakra: Crown
Color: White
Gemstones: Crystal, Diamond
Musical Note: B

. . . Ever since the entering of spirit and soul into matter there
has been a way of redemption for the soul, to make an association
and a connection with the Creator, THROUGH the love FOR
the Creator that is in its experience . . .   440-5

The seventh, or crown, chakra connects us to God, or Source. As its
name suggests, it is located at the top of your head, and it vibrates to
the colors white or violet.

Deep meditation and visualization of connecting with Father Sky,
the stars, and the heavens can facilitate the opening of the crown.
The crown is the place in all of us where all universal and divine love
is downloaded into our being. If we feel down or disconnected from
society, this can often signal that our crown is blocked. Universal love,
peace, and hope are all attributes of this chakra.

The Etheric Bodies

Material conditions are as patterns of those conditions in the
etheric . . .   140-18

Aside from your colored chakra centers and aura, you also have an
infinite field of light that surrounds your physical body and connects
you to the divine. This light can become wider or narrower depending
on your physical vitality and your overall mental and spiritual well-being, so it's important to address these etheric centers in healing work.

Cayce described the field as the aura, yet within the aura there are
different layers to that field known as the etheric bodies.

Source eloquently reminds us that our material world is a mere
reflection of what exists in the unseen etheric realm, and the same principles apply to our bodies. Illness and disease begin first in the etheric
before actualizing on the material plane within our bodies, which is
why healing works to address the unseen energies and shift them to
higher frequencies before they ever reach the material world.

Theoretically the etheric body is only one infinite ball of light that
connects you with the entire universe; however I've always experienced
the etheric light as having three energetic densities or thicknesses, each
relating to body, mind, and spirit. Not surprisingly, Source also describes
three layers around the physical body, referring to these as the spiritual
bodies, which is how we will refer to them for the remainder of this
book. These energetic bodies are your direct link with your Creator and
everything else in the universe.

One of the primary goals of energy work is to remove blockages from
the etheric bodies so you may be more perfectly connected to Source.
When you are healthy and fully functioning, your energy field has the
potential to emanate over twenty-five feet around your physical self.
The challenge we face in our lifetimes is being able to deal with stress in
such a way as not to allow those lower frequency energies to interfere
with experiencing the maximum potential of our energy field. Clearing
the spiritual bodies from blockages allows you to achieve and become
all you can possibly be in your lifetime.

Each layer of your spirit deals with different parts of your existence.
Understanding them can help you on your path and will be an import-

ant part of your healing work regardless of the modality you are using. I really like how Source described the three layers of energy, so we will use the following terms as we move through the next section.

First, know thyself and thy ideal—spiritually, mentally, materially.   3027-2

While Source prefers, in this instance, a different order of terms, I like to start with the material world and then move on to the mental and spiritual realms, so they follow along the lines of body, mind, and spirit.

Material

If the expression is rather in the physical or the material conditions, these find expression in activities in a material expression of same, for the spirit worketh within and through and with every activity of the spiritual expression of an entity in the material plane.   557-3

The term *material* is what Cayce and Source often use to describe your physical body. As long as we are in a three-dimensional shell, all healing must begin here so we can continue to exist on the earth plane.

When I work with people in healing, one of the methods is to place your hands over the person's body and begin to sense the unseen field of energy around them. The material field is the densest part of the field because it is closest to our physical body. You can best sense this field by placing the hands an inch or two above the physical body without touching the actual body.

If you've taken a healing class in the past, particularly Reiki, you learn to move these layers around to get the energy swirling, and the most important goal of any healing would be to enliven the field that is closest to the person's physical body because that is where the unseen blockages are that could eventually lead to dis-ease within the physical person. We will discuss these blockages more as we go through the book.

Cayce and Source understood clearly that the beginning of any healing begins in the body. The Egyptian Energy Healing was created to address specific rituals that would involve fasting and intake of proper foods designed to cleanse the physical person, ridding it of toxicity so that the higher realms could be attained.

In the Egyptian readings, Cayce is not as specific about what these processes are, yet the life readings are filled with practices for healthy living and cleansing that I assume we can take to heart and that, if followed even today, will lead to a healthier lifestyle.

This book will not go into those physical remedies; however there are numerous books already out on this subject, including an incredible work by A.R.E. Research Director, John Van Auken, called *Edgar Cayce on Health, Healing, & Rejuvenation*, which I highly recommend for more details about these methods.

We will instead discuss the unseen blockages in fields around the body and how we can shift and remove those for highest good. Cayce and Source knew that both internal cleansing, combined with healing forces created lasting change in the individual.

Mental

The mind or the mental body is both spiritual (or everlasting) and temporal. Then it is to the mental self. And this makes for confusions if an equal balance is not kept throughout the experience of the entity.   416-10

You can access the mental body by concentrating on the layer of energy that is about six to eight inches above the physical person. We manifest and create from the mental body, and the energy here allows abundance to flow to us. Our emotional issues—good and bad—are holographically stored here, along with our karma with other people—what goes around comes around.

Creative endeavors such as writing, painting, or music are also manifested in the mental body. Blockages in this area literally obstruct our creativity and hinder our ability to attract abundance. Any creative endeavor is a wonderful expression of your soul's divine potential and ability to manifest your God-given talents on the physical plane. That is the function of the mental body. Blockages in this field can hinder our progress, and yet when we work on ourselves, we can rise above much of our karma and transcend to higher ground.

Spiritual

> Keep self well-balanced, and keep the body physically fit, the
> mental body alert, and the spiritual body—give it an opportunity
> to manifest!   342-1

The spiritual body is the part of you that is connected to the life
force, or God. This is the spiritual self—the soul. If the astral is like your
worldly duties and the mental is your education, the causal is your
connection to God, or your spiritual work.

The spiritual field relates to your meditation practices, your prayers,
and your soul contracts. As the above Cayce quote says, it is about your
ability to manifest your life purposes on the physical plane, the lessons
you came here to experience as part of your divine plan.

I believe that all illnesses begin vibrationally in the outer fields of
the spiritual body and vibrate inward toward the physical body. Some
illness may be brought on by day-to-day stresses, such as work, relationship, or financial challenges. Other illness is part of our karma. We
are born with certain energetic blockages that will ultimately manifest
into various diseases that I believe will manifest at specific times to help
teach us lessons we came here to learn. Energy work can address these
blockages, or perhaps lessen the severity of certain situations. Illness
can often be the best thing that ever happens because it can assist you
in opening to your true calling and path in life.

The spiritual body also connects you to your Creator so you can
more readily hear the quiet directions guiding you to your life path
and steps to take to fulfill your highest potential, or the activities that
will bring the greatest happiness and fulfillment in life.

> Hence it is well that its own mental and material and spiritual self
> there be kept that balance.   1770-2

Cayce reminds us repeatedly that the goal is balance, so as you work
with the energy fields around the body, always keep balance in the
forefront of your mind.

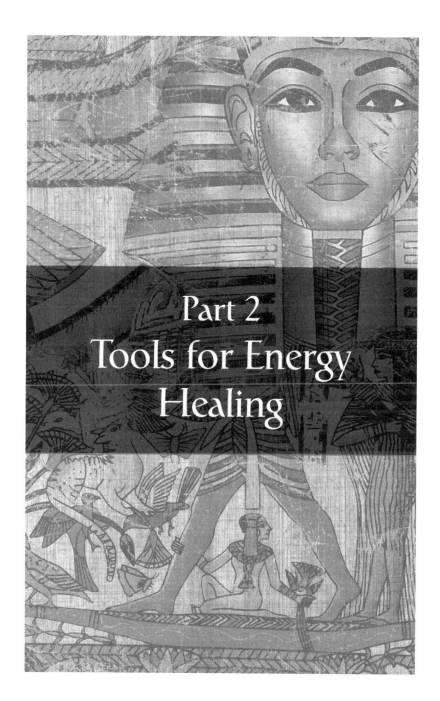

Part 2
Tools for Energy
Healing

For, each soul must come to know its OWN influence and that which is the most helpful. And if it calls then for self to cleanse the body without and within with pure water, or to fast, or to burn incense, or to set about self certain odors or colors of influences, then—as has been given—use these for thine OWN development, but be a seeker and a user of that which thou obtainest. For, not only the hearer but rather the doer gains, in its seeking through to the Infinite forces and influences.   440-12

In the next section we will look at various tools you can use in your healing practice that were recommended by Cayce.

Gemstones

Each element, each stone, each variation of stone, has its own atomic movement, held together by the units of energy that in the universe are concentrated in that particular activity. Hence they come under varied activities according to their color, vibration or emanation.   531-3

Cayce spoke so much about the healing vibrations of gems and stones that I have two books devoted to the topic. Still, I could not write a book on energy healing without including some information on stones as they are my personal favorite tool to use in healing work.

To benefit from the energy of stones, you can put them in the room with you and allow their subtle influences to shift energies that way, or you can wear them in jewelry or carry them in your purse or pocket. Stones have achieved a state of perfection vibrationally speaking, so when one of your chakra centers is not balanced and you introduce a particular stone to that area, the field will begin to shift and attempt to emulate the frequency of the stone you're using.

Since we've spent time discussing chakras and color, let's take a look at what I call the Stones of the Rays, which are tied to the colors in the rainbow spectrum.

Red
Root Chakra
Ruby

The ruby would make for the body that not as something which would be other than the power that self attributes to same, through its actual experience. But the light or reflection from same, worn on hand or body, will enable the body to concentrate in its mental application the greater—through the influences such a stone brings to material expression . . .

. . . In this particular one (the ruby) there is that fitness with that which has been the experience of THIS soul, this entity, through material expression. Hence it is an aid, a crutch to lean upon. But, as has always been given, let it be a stepping-stone; NOT that which thou STANDEST only upon!   531-3

When speaking about colors, ruby is vibrating at the same frequency as the color red, which correlates to the root chakra and therefore grounds the person, exactly as Source suggests in the reading above.

In this case, for example, if I believed my root center was out of balance, I could lie down and actually place the ruby on the area of the body closest to the root chakra and allow the stone to assist with the needed shift.

Orange
Sacral
Carnelian

The omen the body should ever wear on the person is a Maltese cross, or a stone of the agate . . .   500-1

Carnelian is the orange member of the agate family which is why I include the above reading with this entry. Creativity is the attribute of this stone. It will help open up the creative flow and assist you in getting things done. Also, I've heard numerous reports that it assists with allergies and relieves stuffed up sinuses. Napoleon Bonaparte wore an engraved carnelian signet ring to protect him in battle, and carnelian can certainly help you gain courage and strengthen your resolve to face any challenge.

Yellow
Solar Plexus
Citrine

Stones—those of the yellow tint or nature would be the better. These bring the vibrations for more harmonious influence in one who is especially influenced in Mercury, Venus and Mars.

2648-1

Citrine is carrier of the yellow ray and therefore assists with the solar plexus chakra. This gem is called the Merchant's Stone because if you place it in the cash register, your till will grow. Likewise, if you want to increase the flow of money into your life, carry a piece in your purse or pocket and watch the results!

Citrine is a member of the quartz family, as is amethyst. If you heat treat a piece of amethyst, it turns into the yellow citrine, and this is how much of the stone is produced today. Of course, if these stones heat up in nature, that can happen too, although this is more of a rare occurrence. Still, whether heat treated or not, citrine is a personal favorite and one I know you will love using.

Green
Heart
Emerald

(Q) Does it appear that I will sell my emeralds? if so,—
(A) (Interrupting) This again—if it is the choice to, yes. If it is NOT the choice to, it is not NECESSARY in the ACTIVITIES

of the entity—unless it's desirous to be used in other directions!
(Q) If so, when and for how much?
(A) (With a sound or sigh of impatience) We are through!

                                                              1554-7

There are other readings from Source about emeralds, but I include this one here because, quite frankly, it makes me laugh. Source does not put up with people asking silly questions, and I think this reading is a great reminder to us all not to take such trivial matters so seriously in our lives.

Emerald is a member of the beryl family and is incredibly powerful for healing the heart, both physically and emotionally. If you're concerned about spending a lot, don't be. I've found some reasonably priced pieces that are more lapidary grade instead of the clear translucent (and expensive) gem variety.

Place these on the body over the heart, wear them in jewelry, or simply have some in the space where you want to set your healing intentions.

Blue
Throat
Sapphire

Sapphires are members of the corundum family, the same as rubies, and they carry the blue ray, so they are awesome tools for opening up the throat chakra.

I happen to adore sapphires, especially when I was told to wear them after a Vedic astrology reading. In India, people believe that stones can actually rectify weaknesses in the astrological chart, so stones are used as remedies to provide overall support. The concept is similar to the way Cayce and Source explain why certain people should wear certain stones. Cayce's recommendations were almost always relating to past-life influences, and Vedic recommendations are in essence the same because they are implying karma and past-life influences that need healing in the present time. That being said, Source never mentioned sapphires directly, but some of his clients mentioned owning them.

If you're concerned about the cost of procuring a gem-quality sapphire, you can actually purchase a lower grade sapphire to use in healing, or you can also use any of the blue stones you're drawn to for your throat center to help with communication.

Purple
Third Eye
Amethyst

In the choice of stones, do wear the amethyst as a pendant about the neck, as a part of the jewelry. This will also work with the colors to control temperament.   3806-1

Amethyst has the same frequency as the color purple and is, therefore, a wonderful tool to open your third eye. The calming frequencies can also be beneficial, as Source points out in the reading above.

To work with amethyst, you can wear it, as suggested in the reading, or take a chunk and wave it over the energy fields around the body to remove stagnant energy. This is something I show practitioners in my gem healing course, and it's very effective for calming energy fields, removing unwanted influences, and raising the overall frequency.

White
Crown
Crystal

As to the elemental influences having to do with the entity's experience—we find that the crystal as a stone, or any white stone, has a helpful influence—if carried about the body; not as an omen, not merely as a "good luck piece" or "good luck charm" but these vibrations that are needed as helpful influences for the entity are well to be kept close about the body.   2285-1

Crystals are incredibly beneficial to use in healing work because they can amplify any other stone you're working with and move stuck energy. Because they reflect white light, they are wonderful tools for your crown chakra area, helping you open up to your divinity and connect with your Creator.

Next, let's take a look at a few stones Source says we can use specifically to work with our material, mental, and spiritual bodies.

Material = Bloodstone

> There are those to whom the bloodstone brings harmony, and
> less of the tendencies for anger; and so with each.   5294-1

Although Source cites bloodstone as assisting with anger—a mental
issue, I still consider bloodstone's influence more physical because of
the many incredible physical healings I've experienced through the
years with this stone. I believe bloodstone is the most powerful of them
all for addressing certain conditions.

Believed to be the stone under Christ when he was on the cross,
bloodstone is often a dark green color (thanks to chlorite found within)
and has red flecks colored by the grounding iron–based mineral, he-
matite. When placed on the body, these red flecks are often absorbed
into the physical person and can provide incredible transformations for
cancers or any serious condition, but especially with the lungs. After
talking about this on radio shows and in classes for years, I get letters
all the time from readers who have seen this themselves. Try it!

Mental = Topaz

> Then, in choosing the interpretations of the records of those
> things that have their influence or urge—keep the topaz as a stone
> about thee always. Its beauty, its purity, its clarity, may bring to
> thee strength. For this ye have found, and will find oft needed in
> thy dealings with thy problems, and with thy fellow men.
>
> 2281-1

Your mental body is another way of describing the aspect of you that
deals with human emotions and difficulties, karma, and life lessons. The
reading above suggests that this person would benefit emotionally by
the influences of the topaz to assist with creating harmonic frequencies
of cooperation with others.

While certain stones do bring peace to the emotional body, really any stones will shift you into a more positive state of being simply by the fact that stagnant energy will be moved and enlivened and that movement of any kind can lead you to a higher state of being.

Spiritual = Lapis

. . . lapis is not considered a high quality of gem; rather a very low form, but for that indicated in the character of the stone itself, it would be most helpful in creating that vibration which will make for developments of certain characters of demonstrations with any psychic forces or psychic individuals.   440-3

Lapis was mentioned more than any other stone in the life readings. For many people Source pointed out that it was a stone of great spiritual power which would aid meditation and assist in energetically supporting those who had had past lives in Egypt. Additionally, lapis can assist with psychic development, as the life reading above states.

If there were only one stone I would recommend for expanding your spiritual body, lapis would undoubtedly be the best.

Pendulum

As will be and is gradually being understood, each metal, each element even, has its attractions and its repulsions for the other metals or combinations of same in the different degrees, and in different ways and manners. And if used in search for those things hidden, or misplaced, it will be found that oft—in the experience of some individuals—these may be used as a means of locating such. Such is the use of the pendulum.   2431-1

One of my all-time favorite spiritual tools is the pendulum, and I was thrilled, yet not at all surprised, to see that Cayce and Source left us what I believe to be some excellent information about how to best use this tool for spiritual development.

A pendulum is typically a crystal, or some other heavy pointed object, attached to a rope or chain that is used to give yes-or-no answers to simple questions, or in some cases, to assist you with finding lost objects.

When you see those old movies about mesmerists who wave watches in front of their subjects' eyes in order to hypnotize them, that is somewhat how the pendulum swings, so to speak. Because of my fascination with hypnosis, it might be one of the reasons why I'm so fascinated by pendulums.

If you're like me, you probably find that some tools resonate better with you than others. For example, after taking a Tarot card-reading class that lasted two months, I still couldn't get a grasp on how to best offer readings or even to use them at all other than to admire the rich symbolism within the deck. On the other hand, runes are a tool I find quite revealing, helpful, and easy to use. The same is true of the pendulum. I've spent more hours than I'd care to admit holding chains with crystal points and allowing them to show me the right answer to various questions and concerns I've had over the years.

Source wisely tells us that pendulum use is not for everyone:

> To say that there is naught in the use of the pendulum would be in error. To say that each entity could use same would also be in error.   2431-1

Source is absolutely correct. I've taught the pendulum in many of my healing classes over the years, and some people get it right away, while others take a while longer. Of course, if you want to use this tool and it's not working perfectly the first time, practice! There's no reason why you can't improve dramatically over time.

> To make same practical in the experience of an individual, then, is to find—by patient experimentation—those elements that for the individual entity have this attraction.   2431-1

Source discusses patience, and that is a big part of the process because before you can actually get information from the pendulum, you have to train it to give you yes–or–no answers.

One of the best ways to train your subconscious mind to work with the pendulum is by using a diagram like the one I've included below.

How to Train Your Pendulum

1) Hold your pendulum between your thumb and index finger of your dominant hand.

2) Place the point of your pendulum over the circle.

3) Say aloud, "Give me a sign for yes."

4) Wait for the response. The pendulum might swing up and down, or it might make a circle. Whatever it does, make a note of it.

5) Say aloud, "Give me a sign for no."

6) Again, wait for the answer.

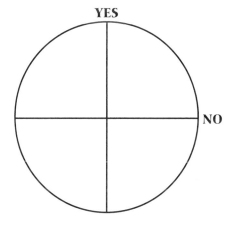

If you're using my diagram, you can see that the "yes" would mean that the pendulum would swing up and down, and the "no" would be back and forth. That might work for you, and it might not. You can try getting the pendulum to swing the way you tell it to, but I've found that it's better if you allow your subconscious and your own energy field to tell you how it wants to communicate.

I have found that when I ask yes-or-no questions, I always get a clockwise spin for a yes, and counterclockwise for a no. Your results may be different, and this is the part that takes a while to master, as Source mentioned earlier. Keep practicing using your pendulum and the diagram. Once you figure out how your pendulum wants to communicate with you, use the following steps to ask questions and find answers:

1) Hold your chain in your dominant hand between your thumb and index finger and allow the crystal or point to hang.

2) Decide what you want to know.

3) Phrase your query in the form of a question using positive language.

4) Ask yes–or–no questions.

5) Wait and see the answer demonstrated by how your pendulum swings.

An example of how you would phrase your question would be to say: "Is it in my best interest to _____?"

Or better yet, say it in the form of a statement:

"It is in my best interest to _____."

Then fill in the blank. If what you're doing is valid, the pendulum will move in the affirmative direction, and if not, you'll get a no answer.

I always ask about my best interest rather than making elaborate requests, because when you work with a pendulum, you are, in essence, asking your Higher Self for guidance, so you want to be clear and positive.

What's most important about the process is to take it seriously and follow what is given. Many times, we receive information we really don't want to hear, so we ignore it or do the exact opposite.

Source gives a great bit of advice on how to get information with the pendulum:

> (Q) In considering the individual entity's work with the pendulum, could you suggest certain elements or minerals with which he—[2431]—should begin experimentation?
> (A) What is he seeking? Water, salt, sand, gold, silver, copper, lead, or what? Begin with whatever he desires to, you see, and work out each one!   2431-1

Because you are using your own body to receive this information, I find that this is the most accurate way to get in touch with what is really best for you at any given time.

As usual, Source seems to share this view:

> To be sure, this information is in a manner very INDEFINITE.

But as has been indicated, it is VERY definite if the individual will take the time, and the experimentation, to FIND, to classify for self, that which is in coordination, or that which is attracted under its usage in the pendulum.   2431-1

Basically, Source is letting us know that if we actually invest the time in doing this and become coordinated with how we use the tool, the results will speak for themselves. That's the same practical advice you could apply to any kind of spiritual process that you want to master. Patience combined with practice yields results.

Pendulums in Healing

In energy healing, the pendulum can be used to see whether the energy fields are vibrant and to identify sources of stuck energy.

We spoke at length about chakra centers, and I mentioned that these are like swirling tornadoes of energy. However, when there is a blockage, the energy does not move at all. So you can place your pendulum over the body, moving it up and down the torso and then see with your own eyes where the blockages are that need to be addressed. For example, the pendulum will be swinging around, full steam ahead over some parts of the body, and then all of a sudden it comes to a dead halt in one or two areas. This shows you with your physical eyes where you need to work to get the energy flowing.

Of course, a lot of healing work is intuitive, as it should be; yet at times, we question ourselves or the validity of psychic information we are given. Tools like the pendulum help us bring the spiritual down to a physical level to reconfirm what we already know. The pendulum can act as your eyes any time you need added confirmation of what is blocked versus what is open. It can also help you reinforce your own intuition, especially if you're doing the healing session by yourself.

Try experimenting with a pendulum. I believe you'll really enjoy it!

Sage Wand

Then take this in the system. To one-half gallon of DISTILLED water add:

8 ounces of common garden sage (dried).   16-1

One of my personal favorite tools to use for energy healing is a dried sage wand. The sage is considered sacred by Native Americans and is wonderful to use for clearing stones or the fields around the body. To work with the sage, you simply light the end of the bundle and wave the smoke over the energy fields to wash away any lower vibrations. Often this is done prior to entering a sacred space or healing ceremony.

I was really excited to find the life reading above, because one of the other ways I've used sage is by making a tea, similar to the way Cayce describes above, and then allowing it to cool and placing gemstones in it so they can be cleansed.

Just as you and I, our stones need an occasional cleaning, and I have used the sage smoke the most often, but in extreme cases where a deep cleansing was needed, I've actually placed amethyst in cool sage tea and after a couple days, the stone was revitalized.

Medicinally speaking, sage can aid digestion and help relieve depression.

Oil

Also the odors which would make for the raising of the vibrations would be lavender and orris root. For these were those of thy choice in the Temple of Sacrifice. They were also thy choice when thou didst walk with those who carried the spices to the tomb.

379-3

Another popular vibrational remedy is essential oil which rapidly shifts the energy fields around the body. Like a lot of people, lavender oil is my personal favorite. Cayce is right about lavender raising vibrations because lavender actually attunes you to the violet ray in the rainbow spectrum while sending restful, healing frequencies to your body. When the body begins to attune, or gets into rapport energetically, with those relaxing waves of lavender, then the body can rest deeply and spiritually; you can open to higher dimensions and greater psychic awareness.

One of my favorite stories is about the essential oil called *Thieves* which is available through Young Living Essential Oils. Apparently back in the days of the bubonic plague, thieves realized that they could pick pockets of the deceased and would not get the plague themselves if they used certain oils. The oil is a blend that includes cinnamon, cloves, lemon, eucalyptus, and rosemary and now has a reputation for strengthening the immune system.

Cayce was a big proponent of using ingestible oils. Later in the book, we will look at oils used in the healing temples, but for now, let's discuss some of the most common oils in the life readings.

Castor Oil

(Q) What oil is best for the system?
(A) The alternation of olive oil and castor oil.
Castor oil should be taken as an ELIMINANT, followed by any saline that cleanses same from system—and should be at least three to five days apart in doses taken, see? Taking about tablespoonful to tablespoonful and a half at a dose, followed with that of a mild saline the next morning.   195-58

Castor oil was mentioned over 2,800 times in the life readings. I've tried it myself after learning about it through Cayce and have found it to be incredibly helpful for assisting with detoxification. I have taken spoonfuls at times, depending on whether I am doing an internal detox, but mostly I use several drops in the bath, so the oil gets into the body through the skin—not exactly like using the hot packs Cayce recommended above, but it's my version of it.

I don't know about you, but once in a while, I feel as if I need a good detox. You know when you feel a little tired or sluggish, and it is then that I try my best to listen to the body and do the detox before anything reaches a critical threshold. Thanks to Cayce, several times when that has happened, castor oil has been one of the items I have turned to the most.

Olive Oil

(Q) What time, and how much olive oil should be taken into
system . . . ?
(A) . . . The OLIVE oil should be a teaspoonful once each day .
. . The olive oil is a food for the intestinal system when taken in
small doses. DO that.   195-58

I've always been a huge fan of olive oil, until recently when I heard
a report on *60 Minutes* about the fact that the Italian mafia currently
controls olive oil exports and has switched pure oil with cheaper products. The reporters tested several well-known brands, and sure enough,
even some of the expensive oils were not real oil.

Sadly, this is becoming a problem with a lot of products. In fact, I was
certain it happened to me because I often use olive oil as a moisturizer
and one bottle made my skin itch. That's when I became wary, so if you
still use the oil, check it out and make sure it's real.

Salt

One of my personal favorite tools to use in healing is salt, although
not all salts are the same. Cayce mentioned several, and we will briefly
review what they are and how you can use them.

Epsom Salt

. . . take an Epsom Salts Bath. Put at least five to six pounds of Epsom Salts in a tub of water, a little above body-temperature, and
gradually add hot water until there is a tub full—or twenty-five
to thirty to fifty gallons of water; with the Epsom Salts dissolved
thoroughly in same . . . Let the body remain in the Epsom Bath
at least twenty to thirty minutes, with the body completely cov-
ered—except the head, of course. Doing these, we will prevent
the temperature, and relieve the tension through the system.
                                                          1807-5

Epsom salt, also known chemically as magnesium sulfate, is incredibly effective at detoxifying the body, eliminating stress and swelling, and giving you an important magnesium boost which some chiropractors have told me that many people sorely need.

I've talked about this in all my books on healing because I am such a huge fan of taking an Epsom salt bath and use this magical substance to cleanse my energy fields after being out all day. When you're around other people and environmental stresses, your energy field can get bogged down with other people's stuff, negativity from outside influences, or even an overabundance of good vibrations that are not your own. Bathing in Epsom salts will allow your energy field to clear so you can get back in touch with the real you again.

This type of bath is especially important for people who are more empathic in nature. Lots of healers have this problem because they are too sensitive to other people's energy, which makes them great healers on the one hand, but can lead to burnout and exhaustion on the other if the practitioners don't have the proper tools to cleanse their own fields after working with others.

If that sounds like you, try this one! It works! Even if you're not a sensitive, I think you'll find it to be amazing.

Table Salt

. . . congestion usually takes toll with the used portions where drosses have been left in system. Then, the relaxations are necessary. Keep the body well balanced in this direction. Not so much of medicinal properties. Occasionally it would be well for the body to use equal parts of cream of tartar and common table salt, with warm water, snuffed up nose, and rinsing the mouth with same, and relax thoroughly, and we will find these conditions clearing up.   257-45

It's not too surprising that Cayce mentioned table salt over five hundred times.

Common table salt is chemically known as sodium chloride. I've mentioned the value of salt many other times but must briefly include it here because common salt is a truly magical substance that is a must-have tool for anyone's healing practice.

If you encircle your healing area or home with salt, it creates a spiritual barrier of protection around you so that no unwelcome influences can come through. Put a salt circle around your massage table, and it sets the intention that only that which is of the light can come through. Likewise, you can walk the exterior perimeter of your home and sprinkle salt around it, and you will be protected. Part of this comes from your own mindfulness as you do the walk, envisioning yourself protected, surrounded by only loving people and situations.

Very powerful!

Breath Work

(Q) Outline breathing exercises best for purifying the body.
(A) Three to five minutes of morning and evening—before an open window, of course—that of rising on the toes with the hands gradually raised above the head at the same time, breathing in deeply. The better way is to breathe first through one nostril, then the other, but this is not easily done—in the beginning. This is the best exercise that may be taken by most any body. For this is not only an exercise of the respiratory system but of all the muscular forces. Watch a cat or a tiger as it stretches. That is the exercise for the muscular forces.

If there is the attempt to vary the breathing from the right to the left nostril, keep same balanced. The left nostril is the spiritual, or the easing; the right nostril is the strength. So keep 'em balanced! Don't get too much strength—that is, don't get more physical strength than you are able to keep balanced through the system. Two to three times through each nostril is the better way, for the expansion of the lungs and for the purifying of circulation by same. Breathe IN through the nostril, OUT through the mouth—when taking such exercise.   2533-3

You may not think of the power of your own breath as a tool you can use in healing, but it is perhaps the best and easiest way to shift your frequencies and what's great about that is you don't have to buy a thing! You simply just have to open yourself up, become mindful and aware of the breathing you're doing, and make sure you aren't holding the breath, which many of us do thanks to the stressors of daily life.

The benefits of proper breathing have been well-documented over the years, so it is not surprising that the life readings contain valuable information, such as the reading above, outlining best practices for working with the breath.

Cayce was one hundred percent spot on in the analysis of the functions of the left and right nostrils. Your right nostril is more masculine in nature and is linked to the left hemisphere of the brain. Your left nostril is more feminine and passive.

I've included a link to a great article from *Yoga International* that discusses the fact that you can learn much about yourself by noticing which one of your nostrils is more open than the other. The goal of any yoga practice is balance, so of course you want both to be open, but the researchers claim that this openness actually fluctuates during the day depending on our activities. That's why Cayce's advice is so wise. You should sit in full concentration a couple times per day and work on breathing in and out of both nostrils simply to exercise the circulation and set the intention that you are consciously seeking that balance.

Another reason why simple breathing exercises are a great way to cleanse and heal our bodies is because your skin is the largest organ in your body. As such, conscious breathing is one of the main ways your skin detoxifies itself.

Let's break down the steps Cayce mentions above so we can do this ourselves. I am not going to be a stickler about whether you choose to stand on your toes and put your head out a window. I believe the intent is to make sure you're in an area with good ventilation and free of pollutants.

I live in Texas, and unfortunately, our air quality can often be horrific, particularly in the summer. I think Cayce would be shocked to see the world today. But that's another story . . . The point of the exercise is to begin breathing in a more conscious way because the breath heals the body physically, and while doing so, you will receive the results in added feelings of peace and harmony that will enable you to deal with the world around you in a brighter way.

Exercise

If you'd like, stand up and rise up to the tips of your toes. If it's not possible to do that, then simply find a place where you can be quiet and still for a few minutes, even if you're sitting in a comfortable chair.

Place your finger over your right nostril. Take a deep breath in through your left nostril. Exhale out of your mouth. Repeat this practice two more times. Release your right nostril. Good job!

Next, place your finger over your left nostril. Take a deep breath in through your right nostril. Exhale out of your mouth. Repeat this practice two more times. Release your left nostril. Great!

How does that feel? I think Cayce is right about the fact this is tough to do at first. There are a lot of pollutants and allergens in the air that affect people. Sometimes it's hard to clear those passageways at first. I've been doing a lot of breath work lately, particularly in my yoga classes, and it's really helping. Lately I've incorporated these Cayce techniques of concentrating on one nostril at a time and have found this to be quite helpful for restoring a feeling of equilibrium to my system. It's quite energizing as well.

Since he recommends doing this twice a day, I like to do this first thing in the morning and right before bed. If you're having a stressful day at work, this is also an awesome time to do the exercise. In life, one of the main tools to help you get through anything is to remember to breathe. It's free and doesn't require anything but our attention.

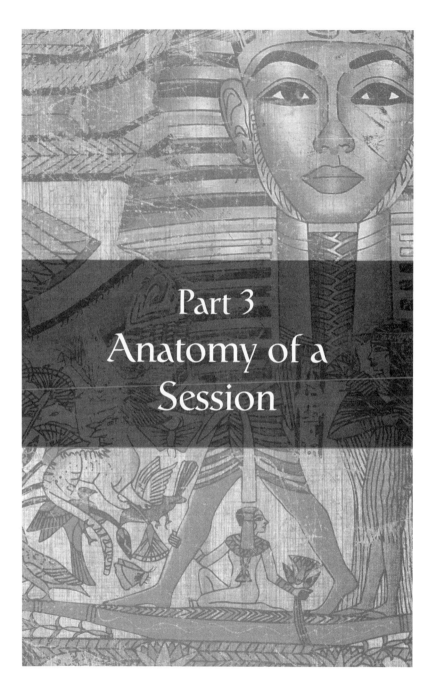

Part 3
Anatomy of a
Session

Healing Ethics

There has also come a teacher who was bold enough to declare himself as the son of the living God. He set no rules of appetite. He set no rules of ethics, other than "As ye would that men should do to you, do ye even so to them" . . .   357-13

Before we go any further, it's important to discuss the "ethics" of healing. This is one of the most debated and controversial subjects of any healing work and throughout the years, I have developed my own thoughts on the subject.

Years ago, when I hosted a radio talk show, a woman called in and told me her son was dying of throat cancer and she hoped that I could help. I heard the desperation in her voice as she explained he had an inoperable tumor and she wanted to know if I would come see him. Based on the details of the conversation, I intuitively felt that she did not have his permission, so I told her I would not come out unless she had actually talked to him and he agreed to see me. Every soul has its own path, and it is important for people to make their own choices in life, regardless of what anyone else wants.

A few days later, she called my office and told me her son wanted to see me, so I went to the house. I will never forget this experience as long as I live. When I walked in, I could immediately see the enormous tumor and sadly, it was obvious he was in tremendous pain. The tumor blocked his windpipe and breathing was a chore.

Once I was in his presence, I still did not have a good feeling this was really what he wanted. A lot of times our family and friends can make us do things we don't want to do, and I wanted to reconfirm I was welcome before I intruded on his space. I introduced myself and said something like, "Do you really want to do this? If you do, that's fine; if not, that's okay too, because I respect your wishes and want you to feel totally comfortable with the process. I believe in miracles, and I believe it is possible that any situation can be turned around if you want it to be. I also believe in your right to choose whether this is your time to go, and if so, I honor that too."

He said yes, he wanted to heal. This is what he told me with his conscious mind—out of his mouth—as his mother watched.

I still had a strange feeling about this, but I decided to do as he asked and began attempting to send him energy. The only problem was the fact that nothing was happening. No energy was coming from my hands. I got a little panicked. I was not about to stand there and pretend to be giving a healing. I kept trying and wondering what to do next.

About the time I was about to give up and tell him and his mom that the session was not working, to my surprise, his image popped into my mind. This startled me at first because in my mind's eye, he looked totally healthy—so much so, I almost didn't recognize him. I assumed this was what he looked like before the cancer.

Within my mind, I said, "Hello. What can I do for you?"

He said, "I don't want to do this. I'm just doing it for my mom."

"Okay," I said, "I totally understand and respect that."

My hands were still stone cold, and I happened to hear his labored breathing. I felt bad for him because it was truly clear he was suffering terribly. Then I had an idea. "Would you want me to help you breathe easier so you can be more comfortable?"

"Can you do that?" he asked.

"Yes. I can at least try if you'd like," I replied.

"Okay," he said.

Incredibly, the split second he agreed to receive help breathing, my hands lit up and energy began to flow.

So, what happened? I changed my intent, and instead of asking the physical person or the "material person" as Cayce might call it, I asked the spiritual person or the soul, also known as the Higher Self. To me, that is the aspect of the person which must be consulted when asking for permission because in real life we are so stressed out and influenced by the conditions around us.

I've been working as a past-life regressionist for a long time now and once in a while, somebody wants to come for a session and bring someone along with them. If possible, I always try to get the person to rethink that request because there are things that come up which are so deeply personal to the soul that having anyone else present can be a real distraction and prevent the person from receiving the healing or outcome he was meant to have.

In the case of this dear man, having his mother around was wonderful on the one hand because she loved and supported him, comforted him, and kept him company during his final hours, and yet it had to have been horrible to face the thought of losing her child. It was that energy which was holding him here and preventing him from going on to the next world. As it turned out, I wound up doing one more session for him with pain relief and comfort as the goal of the healing, and soon afterward, he passed away. During this time, I also worked with his mother to help her let go and heal from his death.

When all is said and done, we have to understand that in life, no matter how much we want to save people and keep them with us, each person chooses when it is time to live and when it is time to die.

Why do I share this story? Because it's a great example of the fact that we are not in charge. We are channels of energy. Nothing more.

Source constantly reminded people that our goal should always be to be a channel of the divine to assist our fellow beings, as in the following reading:

> Not by any great deed, not by any act that may appear other than as a natural consequence in the experience of the entity, but the innate and purposeful desire to be a channel through which others may know more and more—as self may—of the relationship to the Creative Force.   2175-1

Once you train as a healer, you'll often notice your hands will heat up and you'll start sending energy the moment you step into a room. That's a real indication that you are following the instructions of Source and being a channel for others. When this happens to me, I assume that someone nearby needs healing. A lot of times, I have no idea who it is, so I go into my mind, say a silent prayer, and ask that the energy go to anyone who needs it and that Higher Will be done. Asking for the Higher Will or alignment with Creator is key.

Intention

Each soul enters that awareness in this material experience that
the entity may glorify the Creative Force, or God, in the entity's
relationship with others.   2550-1

Once you are able to let go, let God, and release your personal
attachment to any outcome, then you're on your way to having a
successful healing session. As long as your intentions are pure, open
yourself up to receive and know that the Creative Force, as Cayce called
it, will do the rest.

What should our intentions be? According to Source, we should
strive to be a blessing to others in all we do:

(Q) How can I extend the borders or my consciousness to achieve
greater spiritual development and illumination?
(A) Open thy heart, thy mind to the prayer indicated: HERE
AM I, EMPTIED OF ALL MY OWN DESIRE; SELFLESS
BEFORE THEE, O GOD. FILL THOU MY HEART AND
SOUL WITH THE PURPOSE TO BE A CHANNEL OF
BLESSING TO SOMEONE TODAY.   3654-1

In the above reading, Source shares an amazing example of what
our intentions should be during any healing interaction with someone—emptiness, devoid of ego, a state of willingness and permitting.
Open your heart and allow Source energy to bless another person. The
spirit of helpfulness is always required when you're sending energy to
another person.

We want to be helpful and we most likely hope the energy we give
will be well-received and used for the highest good of the person,
whether that be for physical healing, emotional stability, or greater
peace in that person's life. Still, we must remember as healers that even
if people do accept energy from us, it is literally none of our business
what they choose to do with it. That sounds harsh, I know, but it's true.
You may want certain things to happen, but it is up to that person to
decide what his journey is and how your assistance will be used.

Let's consider this another way. Think about Christmastime, or birthdays, when one is giving or receiving gifts. Once you give gifts to people, do you stand over them and watch to make sure they do what you would do with them? No, of course not. You give it and then it's up to them, right? The same needs to happen in healing.

In the case of the cancer patient, I had the benefit of receiving input as to what he was going to do with the energy when his Higher Self allowed me to help him with his personal comfort, but a lot of times you won't know what your efforts are doing specifically.

The past few years, I've received a ton of requests for distance healing for clients in different parts of the world. Some had accidents; others were fighting cancer; and some received energy for emotional support concerning pressing issues they were faced with at the time. Normally, I receive letters from the folks letting me know what is going on, but even then, all I can do is get out of my own way and allow the energy to flow through.

The main goal is my *intent*, which is always that the healing is being sent for the highest good of all concerned and that the person will use the energy for whatever he most needs at the time. After working with clients for so many years, I have concluded that the permission you need to seek before doing any healing must come from the soul and not from the ego consciousness of the recipient.

A great statement of intention to say to yourself before giving any healing is the following which I've successfully used for years:

"You are free to accept or reject this healing. May Higher Will be done."

In summary, you are always completely in charge of your own unconscious mind. You and your client are responsible, at least at an unconscious level, for how much energy will be exchanged. That is a function of the Higher Self. Do your best with the intention of assisting your fellow beings and know that all is well!

Prayer

And thy prayer should ever be: "THY WILL, O LORD, NOT MINE, BE DONE IN AND THROUGH ME."   2390-1

Speaking of intentions, nothing sets the tone of your intentions while creating a sacred space to do your work better than a simple prayer. I absolutely love the prayer Source gives us in the above reading, for what else could we ever ask than to be a conscious channel for intention?

Before you do any healing, it is best to say a prayer for the recipient. What you say, how you say it, whether the prayer is spoken aloud or to yourself is irrelevant. What matters is your intention to send a blessing for the recipient's benefit. I like saying my prayers silently most of the time when I'm working with my clients on the massage table. Then again, once in a while, I intuit that the prayer will comfort the person, and when that's the case, I say something aloud. Offering an audible prayer gives comfort to people and lets them know that there is divine assistance contributing to the session and that only the highest frequencies of love and light are working with you.

Source provides us with assurances that you are spiritually protected in the following reading:

> . . . know that the self, the ego, the I, is in accord with, is aware
> of, the divine protection that has and does come to each and every
> soul that fulfills its mission in any experience.   442-3

Over the years after working with so many people in hypnosis, I've discovered for a fact that the presence of a guide or angel who accompanies someone on his journey makes all the difference in the person's ability to feel safe and be fully capable of achieving the outcome he wants during the session.

Why would audible prayers or acknowledging the higher power comfort someone so much? For a couple of reasons:

First, I believe we don't want to go it alone in life or on the spiritual path. We need each other, and on some level, we want someone we trust by our side to accompany us on the journey—a friend to assist, whom we can bounce things off of, so to speak.

Second, often in hypnosis, the people will listen to what the guide or angel tells them to do before they will listen to themselves. Haven't you ever found that to be the case? We often know what is for our highest and best, and yet talking to old, trusted friends and listening to what they say, especially if they've known us for a long time, often validates our decisions and makes us feel okay about taking certain steps.

Along those lines, an angel comes across as an authority. When I guide my clients, I let them know that the guide or angel who shows up for them has always been by their side, has always had their back, and knows everything there is to know about them—perhaps things they did not even know about themselves. With that kind of an ally by your side, how could you go wrong? You couldn't! And that is a great feeling!

In addition, I believe our souls are steeped with the traditions from centuries of incarnations filled with dormant memories of ancient rituals. Going through processes and communicating with the divine is commonplace on a soul level. It feels familiar to us, and there is something extra comforting about the ritual of having a celestial being by our side.

If, and when, you do energy work for people in person, I think you'll find it's a quiet process, so use your intuition to decide if you want to say something out loud. Hopefully you have a chance to speak to your clients and know before you begin if they are people who enjoy working with Jesus or Mother Mary, or if they prefer to think of the divine as more of an angelic being or guide. Sometimes you'll find that it isn't possible to get the answer. Just do your best!

Everybody's different, and for those on the spiritual path, they are often more eclectic in their beliefs in terms of religion. Many believe in spirit guides and angels rather than a specific deity or the idea of calling upon Jesus himself. I've worked with several people who have had extremely negative childhood experiences in the church who now want nothing to do with traditional religious terms and figures. As healers, we must respect our clients' views if they differ from our own and use terms that make them more comfortable during the session.

Affirmations

In giving the affirmations, let them be prepared in such a manner that they will be preserved by those to whom they may be sent.

281-25

One of the things I teach my energy-healing students is to always open a healing session with a prayer for the person receiving the healing. Several times over the years I've actually had people say they are not comfortable with the word *prayer*.

Another term we can use for prayer is *affirmation*. I am a big fan of using affirmations to help us phrase what we want in positive language that allows the universe to bring us our highest and best.

Dictionary.com defines an affirmation as:

"The assertion that something exists or is true."

Truth is the key in using affirmations. We speak with authority as if the condition we want is already present and already true. That's why affirmations are so powerful.

One of my personal favorite affirmations is:

"*I am healthy, body, mind, and spirit.*"

I say this over and over to myself and can often feel the cells in my body rearranging themselves as I declare what is true.

The idea that we are working with truth is why affirmations are so powerful. They are statements that when said with belief, and spoken in the present tense, can come true for you, even if that current condition is not how things are in your current three-dimensional reality. You've heard the statement "fake it until you make it," right? That's exactly how affirmations work. In a sense, that's exactly what we're doing when we offer a prayer for somebody. We are asking that a state of perfection come into being for the person, even if that's not how things are in the moment.

Amazingly, and yet not too surprisingly, Source also discussed affirmations in the life readings and provided an entire set of nine "affirmations for healing" to a group of light workers:

The FIRST: LORD, THOU ART MY DWELLING PLACE. ABIDE THOU, O GOD, IN THE TEMPLE OF MY BODY, THAT IT MAY BE WHOLLY AS THOU WOULD HAVE IT.

The SECOND: LET THE JOY OF THE LORD FILL MY MIND, MY BODY, QUICKENING THE SPIRIT, THAT THE DEEDS THAT ARE DONE MAY BE ACCEPTABLE IN HIS SIGHT.

The THIRD: LORD, KEEP THOU MY WAYS. LET ME FIND JOY AND PLEASURE IN MANIFESTING SUCH A LIFE THAT IT MAY GIVE HOPE AND HELP AND CHEER TO OTHERS.

The FOURTH: LORD, THE MAKER OF HEAVEN AND EARTH, THE GIVER OF THE CHRIST IN THE HEARTS OF MEN, QUICKEN THOU THE SPIRIT WITHIN, THAT THY LIGHT, THY LOVE, MAY BE MANIFEST-ED THROUGH ME.

The FIFTH: LORD, THOU ART MY REDEEMER. IN THE CHRIST DO WE SEEK TO KNOW THEE THE BETTER. LET LOVE AND HEALTH, LET JOY AND PROSPERITY OF THE LORD QUICKEN MY WAYS.

The SIXTH: LORD, THOU ART THE GIVER OF ALL GOOD AND PERFECT GIFTS. MAY THE LIGHT OF THY COUNTENANCE IN CHRIST SHINE UPON ME NOW, MAKING FOR THE MANIFESTATIONS OF THE LOVE THOU HAST PROMISED IN HIM.

The SEVENTH: LORD, MAKER OF HEAVEN AND EARTH AND ALL THEREIN. LET THE LOVE OF THE CHRIST BE MY GUIDE, THAT MY BODY, MY MIND, MAY BE WHOLE IN THEE: AND THUS BE THE CHAN-NEL OF A BLESSING TO OTHERS.

The EIGHTH: LORD, THOU ART MY DWELLING PLACE. QUICKEN THE SPIRIT WITHIN ME THAT THOU MAY HAVE THY WAY WITH ME, THAT I MAY BE THE GREATER CHANNEL OF BLESSINGS TO OTHERS.

The NINTH that as written over the door of the Temple Beautiful:
PARCOI [?] SO [?] SUNO [?] CUM [?]. LORD, LEAD

THOU THE WAY. I COMMIT MY BODY, MY MIND, TO
BE ONE WITH THEE.   281-25

The group wondered if these affirmations were for specific people
and how they should be used:

> (Q) In referring to the affirmations, in same reading, was it meant
> that just the nine affirmations given in that reading were to be
> prepared and preserved by those to whom they were sent, or all
> of our affirmations?
> (A) All. For each affirmation should, and does, fill a place, a
> purpose, in the minds, in the hearts, of those that—through
> concerted and consecrated effort—seek to be a channel and to
> be one with Him.   281-26

As Cayce so eloquently stated above, the affirmation or prayer is
something that can be used for anyone. I believe we should all use
our guidance to the best of our abilities when sending prayer, but the
bottom line goes back to what we discussed earlier about intention.
Your intention for any healing is for the recipients to be happy, peaceful,
and at ease; so regardless of the words you use, say something or think
something meaningful that embodies the spirit of the well wishes you
are sending them and know that all is well.

Spirit Guides, Ascended Masters, and Angels

> (Q) Did that mean my father, spirit guide, or He I call Father
> above all—God?
> (A) Through the father to the God, yes.   900-77

I always like to enlist the help of spiritual beings in all healing sessions. There are unlimited guides and angels you can call in to assist
you or your clients.

It we look at the above reading, I would assume Source and Cayce do
not necessarily believe in any guides except Christ and God. However,
there are good reasons for working with guides, because all people
are different, and while they are all asking for help from the divine,

the way that help shows up for them in the realm of their imaginations or internal thoughts can be different for everyone. For people to get the most out of the work, they often need the help of a trusted guide.

Over the years, there have been countless angels, guides, and helpers who have showed up when people needed them. I was stunned to see how many of the guides I've worked with were actually mentioned by Cayce in the life readings.

Jesus

So, as ye have found, so as ye may find in thy experiences in the present, doubt and fear are cast away when the thoughts are lifted to the hope that comes in the Cross, even in the Cross of Jesus!

2272-1

I love Jesus and there is no better individual to assist in healing. When you call him, he always shows up and is incredibly helpful and amazing. When I call on Jesus, I typically envision him standing on my left side. Why? I have no idea, but he always stands there and has for many years.

Don't let this influence you too much. Just allow him to show up and see where he appears and what he does. Know it's in divine order.

Mother Mary

. . . much of those activities might be indicated that brought about those later relationships with Mary, the mother of Jesus.

1010-17

Another personal favorite is Mother Mary. I've worked with her quite a bit through the years, and she shows up quite often in sessions. You may have your favorite internal image of her, and that is always the best to use. For me, the ideal Mary is the Virgin de Guadalupe with bright colors all around her.

Typically, Jesus and Mary come together to assist and while Jesus stands on my left, Mary stands on my right. Their loving presence is incredibly helpful.

White Brotherhood

Thus this entity, Josie, was selected or chosen by those of the Brotherhood—sometimes called White Brotherhood in the present—as the handmaid or companion of Mary, Jesus and Joseph, in their flight into Egypt.   1010-17

The White Brotherhood is another amazing group of guides who can assist you in healing. I've worked with them extensively through the years. Source provided the best definition of this collective consciousness I've seen:

(Q) Were the Essenes called at various times and places Nazarites, School of the Prophets, Hasidees, Therapeutae, Nazarenes, and were they a branch of the Great White Brotherhood, starting in Egypt and taking as members Gentiles and Jews alike? (A) In general, yes. Specifically, not altogether. They were known at times as some of these; or the Nazarites were a branch or a THOUGHT of same, see? Just as in the present one would say that any denomination by name is a branch of the Christian-Protestant faith, see? So were those of the various groups, though their purpose was of the first foundations of the prophets as established, or as understood from the school of prophets, by Elijah; and propagated and studied through the things begun by Samuel. The movement was NOT an Egyptian one, though ADOPTED by those in another period—or an earlier period—and made a part of the whole movement.   254-109

One of my favorite books is *MAP—The Co-Creative White Brotherhood Medical Assistance Program* by Machaelle Wright. In the book, she shows you how to call this team in to assist with a variety of issues. If so guided, the White Brotherhood is wonderful to assist you with healing.

Archangel Michael

Michael is an archangel that stands before the throne of the Father . . . Michael is the lord or the guard of the change that comes in every soul that seeks the way, even as in those periods when His manifestations came in the earth.   262-28

Michael is the archangel of protection. I work with him daily. There is never a single day of my life when I do not ask for his protection and guidance. He is a rock and will encircle your work in protective and loving light, fending off any unwanted influences and ensuring that only that which is of the Light enters your healing area. I imagine Archangel Michael with a huge sword, cutting off any unwanted influences, and then surrounding me or the client with a circle of high frequency light. No darkness can penetrate this protective shield. He is amazing!

Michael is an important part of the life readings. Source brought Michael through several times when profound healing was needed.

Archangel Raphael

Raphael is the archangel of healing, so he is an obvious choice to assist in sessions for self and others. He is compassionate and assists individuals in opening to the healing light available to us all.

Archangel Gabriel

(Q) Was there any appearance of the angel Gabriel in the home?
(A) In the temple when she was chosen, in the home of Elizabeth when she was made aware of the presence by being again in the presence of the messenger or forerunner.   5749-7

In the reading above, Source was asked about the life of Mary and how her special purpose was revealed. Because Gabriel is the messenger of God, it makes sense this powerful archangel was present at the time Mary's gifts were revealed.

In healing, you can call Gabriel in and he will assist in helping messages be received for the highest good of all concerned.

Archangel Uriel

Uriel is the archangel of wisdom. His name means Light of God, and he often shows up to bring clarity and serenity to healing sessions.

Archangel Ariel

(Q) Who is Halaliel?
(A) . . . Halaliel is the one who from the beginning has been a leader of the heavenly host, who has defied Ariel, who has made the ways that have been heavy—but as the means for the UN-DERSTANDING. [Isaiah 29th chapter?]   254-83

Ariel is the archangel of nature and the natural world. Sadly, we are becoming so connected to our devices these days that we often over-look the healing power of nature. Especially during these times, Ariel is quite supportive to have in healings.

Archangel Jophiel

I've been working with Jophiel lately because he is the angel of artists. Personified as Beauty of God, he will help you find beauty in all things and reconnect to nature. He vibrates to a yellow color and is very peaceful. Call on him to connect to your creativity or for help with beautifying any area or natural setting.

Archangel Azrael

(Q) Can you contact Azul [Azool? Azrael? Azazel?] for me?
(A) Demetrius—Michael; Azul—no.
(Q) You cannot?
(A) Cannot.
(Q) Why?
(A) There are barriers between this body and Azul, as produced

by that between Demetrius and between Michael.   2897-4

Azrael is the archangel of transitions, sometimes referred to as the Angel of Death. He helps people who are grieving to let go, advises grief counselors, and assists souls in transitioning into the next world. If you are dealing with grief or loss, call on him to help.

In the reading above, Source was asked about Azul which some speculate was a reference to Azrael, and Source was unable to make contact with him.

Archangel Chamuel

Chamuel is the archangel of peace. Call on him to bring feelings of peace and calm to your life and to alleviate fears.

Since we are bombarded by so much fear and negativity these days, Chamuel will help you see the truth and rise above lower vibrations.

Enoch

. . . Enoch walked with God, became aware of God in his movements . . .   1158-5

Enoch was the great grandfather of Noah and a prominent figure in the Bible with whom I have worked extensively in healing through the years to assist in creative endeavors and overall spiritual support.

Saint Germain

(Q) Who are the Masters directly in charge? Is Saint Germain— [Comte de (c. 1710 c. 1780)?]—
(A) (Interrupting) Those that are directed by the Lord of lords, the King of kings, Him that came that ye might be one with the Father.
(Q) Is Saint Germain among them? . . .
(A) These are all but messengers of the Most High . . .

(Q) Is Saint-Germain among them?
(A) When needed.   254-83

Saint Germain, carrier of the Violet Flame, appears in my healing sessions from time to time. Earlier we discussed that Edgar Cayce recommended the ultra–violet light to clients over the years.

Another way to benefit from the violet color is to call in the Violet Flame of Saint Germain. To access this, you will use the power of your inner world and imagination to envision a violet flame that burns up from the ground and swirls around your entire body while raising your frequency. The flame releases karma and clears your energy centers, while making you feel refreshed.

You can also call on Saint Germain and allow him to assist in raising frequencies of a room by casting the Violet Flame over and around the healing area. This flame is incredibly high frequency and will set the tone for your session. I love it!

Buddha

. . . Now, there may be obtained such as is the spirit of Buddha,
or Buddhism in its CRYSTALLIZED form . . .   311-3

Mentioned twenty–six times in the life readings, Buddha energy represents compassion for all beings and a state of perfection and highest order that we all aspire to become. Buddha does not show up in healings as often as the others I've mentioned, but once in a while, if you're guided to bring him in, or if you see him in your mind's eye, it likely means you're tapping in to the person's past lives in Asia. Go with it and know that Buddha is a wonderful ally to align with in any healing session.

Speaking to the Guides

Once you decide which guide you want to work with, how do you get that one's attention?

To call in divine help, your next step is choosing the right words to set the tone for your session and to enlist the assistance of the appropriate guide or helper. If I am guided to do so, oftentimes my audible prayer is a simple one. I say something like: *"We call in John's (or whatever the person's name is) guides, angels, and ascended masters as we begin this healing today and ask that Higher Will be done."* What happens next is interesting. I will often begin to see or sense the various guides who show up, either in my mind's eye, or I might perceive visible light in the room, smell roses or other pleasant fragrances, or perhaps objects such as my gems and stones will start moving around. In whatever way they choose to show up, these magical moments let me know that I have indeed contacted the divine.

Be Open to Receive

Over the years, I've found that most people are not largely aware of which guides work with them, and that is okay. This is where your intuition must come in by allowing a guide or an angel to appear in your mind's eye. Trust your intuition and know that the vision or gut feeling or however you receive that information is in divine order.

If I am saying my prayers silently, I simply ask that whoever is most important to the person, in terms of divinity, comes to assist the healing while supporting the highest good and brightest outcome. Then I do not have an attachment to the results or who might show up. I've done healings where Jesus or Archangel Michael shows up, and I simply feel their presence.

Other times, I sense that the energy is more of a personal guide or perhaps a deceased family member who is lending support. The idea is to be open to what comes through and to do all with the helpful intentions of benefiting the person or group receiving the healing.

After the session, if the person you're working with wants to know what you've picked up during the session, you can reveal who came to you. You might not feel comfortable doing so, and believe me, I get that! When I first started as a practitioner, I often felt like much of what came to me sounded silly, but the more I trusted the information and began delivering it, the more confirmation I received. Trust yourself and go for it!

Next, we will do a short exercise that you can use to contact your guides of choice.

Calling in Your Guides for Healing

To give you an idea of how to work with guides, I'd like to share a little exercise you will hopefully find helpful. I've done this for myself and used variations with clients over the years with great results.

Some years ago, I began to notice that Mary and Jesus would appear in my mind's eye during healings with other people. This was a wonderful surprise, and I always enjoyed sharing their energy.

In order to attune myself better for healings, I started a little protection/prayer process for self-healing in the evenings before bed.

I will present this process here with the guides I use the most, but feel free to include any guides you enjoy working with the best. You can do this exercise anytime, but I prefer calling in my guides just before going to sleep because they can give you messages and work with your subconscious mind overnight, which can be super helpful. Let's say you have a challenge you can't figure out what to do. Just hold that concern in your mind as you work with the guides and know by morning, new light and energy will come to you and you will be able to easily resolve whatever the situation is, or you will receive directions on how to do so. It's amazing what we can accomplish in the dream state! That said, if you prefer to use this during a power nap, go for it! This works any time. Let's get started!

Exercise

Go ahead and lie down on your bed, or in a comfortable space. Close your eyes, and imagine you are calling Mother Mary to your right side. Feel her loving presence as she joins you. Very good.

Next, imagine Jesus joins you and stands next to you on your left side. Feel the love he has for you.

Next, Archangel Michael floats down from above and appears with his sword at the foot of the bed.

Once those three are in place, go ahead and ask Archangel Michael to cut cords between you and the outer world. Imagine you can feel a tremendous sense of relief and new energy as you shut the world off for sleep and take this time now to go within. Good job.

Next, notice that Michael is casting a protective, healing light around you. You may want to notice if it's a white light or a golden light or if there are any colors. Good job. Notice that this light surrounds you and protects you. You feel calm and relaxed.

Next, invite Enoch to stand at your headboard and notice him floating down from above, while Archangel Uriel floats over you, and Archangel Ariel arrives, floating under you.

Take a moment and notice if there are any other helpful beings of love and light who wish to join you, and if so, imagine that they float in now. Very good.

Imagine that this group of amazing beings is sending you loving light and lifting any unwanted influences from you, transmuting any lower frequencies into a bright, healing light. Feel the unconditional love and high regard these loving beings have for you. Imagine you can send love back to them. Allow them to tell you anything you need to hear, or you can take this time to ask a question and know that by morning, you will have the appropriate answer.

Now imagine you can bathe in unconditional love and light and carry this energy with you, now and always.

This process takes about ten seconds and is really energetically uplifting. Try it and I think you'll find you're left not only with a deep feeling of great peace and healing but also with a sense that you are divinely guided and protected so you can fall to sleep safely and soundly.

You can also call in this same set of guides when working with others by seeing them surrounding the person receiving the healing. Allow them to work with you to brighten up the healing session.

Try it! It works! Then see what other energies you can work with who bring you healing and peace.

Channeling Energy, Messages, and Symbols

"LORD OF MIGHT, OF POWER, OF LIGHT, KEEP THOU THY SERVANT, THY CHILD, IN THE WAY THOU WOULD HAVE IT GO! DIRECT THE WAYS, THE THOUGHTS, THE CARES, IN THE WAYS THAT MAKE FOR THE CHANNELS OF THY LIGHT TO THY CHILDREN EVERYWHERE."   1222-1

Energy healing and working with guides is an extension of channeling. What is channeling? According to Dictionary.com, channeling is defined as: "The practice of professedly entering a meditative or trancelike state in order to convey messages from a spiritual guide."

There are three things you will channel as a healer: energy, messages, and symbols. Let's take a quick look at all three.

Channeling Energy

> . . . awaken that within self that may be the more helpful, that
> will make self the greater channel for others . . .   275-39

In most energy healing systems, one of the ways you convey healing to other people is by sending it through the hands. In Reiki, people receive attunements to open up their energetic fields so they can bring forth the flow of the divine. When this happens, energy begins to move through the hands into the other person, and for most healers, you can feel when it's working.

Channeling Messages

> Hence through the experiences of the entity in the present so-
> journ we have found that not only in its own land but in others it
> has been called into service to act in the capacity of one to bring
> even material as well as mental and spiritual messages to his
> peoples. These become again then a part of the entity's activities
> in the present sojourn . . .   257-201

Once the energy flows, often there is a vision, an audible message, or a gut feeling about something that needs to be relayed to the other person. The challenge, when this happens, is to have the confidence to pass the information on and to trust your intuition.

During the days in Egypt, prophets assisted others by relaying such messages. One woman was told she served in that capacity in the Egyptian healing temple:

> (Q) [993]: I would appreciate as much information concerning
> the Temple Beautiful as would be of help to me. I have a great
> inner urge to know more about this Temple and its purpose to
> man at this time. Does this Temple not have a close connection

with Destiny? If so, please give.

(A) As the entity was the prophetess to those, it WOULD make the indication to the entity of a definite association or connection with destinies. But Destiny, as ye have studied and as ye have learned: God hath not willed that any soul should perish but hath with each temptation provided a way of approach. Hence man with his free will makes for whether the body is AS the temple of the living God or the Temple Beautiful, with its various stations as represented in the various phases of His experience; as is shown in the body itself in ALL of those urges as arise through emotions, through mind, through association, through puri-fying, through consecration, through determination, through knowledge, through the attributes that become a portion of same. As ye have seen in that thou hast given, may give, that led the many, that opened the way to many, it, the temple, thy temple, thy body, thy mind, thy portion of the God-Consciousness may be aroused and awakened to the abilities within self to assist in those becoming aware of the necessity of arousing to the destinies of the body, the mind, the soul.   281-25

Cayce again mentioned the connection of body, mind, and soul and how these prophets were instrumental in helping others.

When you think about it, all of us channel messages every day. Hav-en't you ever had a friend who felt down, and you somehow tuned in, said the right thing, and was told how much that helped? Or perhaps you've been on the receiving end of such helpfulness. Even simple in-teractions that we often choose to downplay can be connected to the divine when we are tuned in to helping each other.

Cayce gave another reading to remind someone how helpful kind words can be:

(Q) [560]: May I have a message bearing upon that period of time in the Temple Beautiful that may be helpful to me in this experience?
(A) Thou in thine office ever was as the one that tended, gath-ered, comforted those as they passed from station or phase or experience. In encouraging, in comforting, know that thou in

thine service now may give that encouraging word, that aid, that comfort, by the touch of thy hand, by the sound of thy voice, by the SURENESS of thy purpose, by the centralizing of thy ideals in Him.   281-25

Remember that even an encouraging word can be the best gift you can ever offer someone and that our words can, in fact, be healing. Be the blessing for someone else by speaking what's in your heart.

Channeling Healing Symbols

Once we begin looking at and working with Edgar Cayce's Egyptian Energy Healing, I will show you some healing symbols Cayce mentioned that create energy when you send them to other people.

So, what are symbols in healing? I like to define them as "shortcuts for the subconscious mind." Symbols are visual pictures that represent our intentions. We talked earlier about the importance of intentions. Rather than offering a long description, saying a prayer, using affirmations, spelling something out, or trying to explain with great detail what the intention is, the symbol allows your mind to go right to the heart of any matter in a nanosecond.

Modern society is filled with symbols. In today's world, with cell phones and text messages, we are constantly bombarded by more symbols than ever before in history. Thanks to emojis, you don't even have to write out a full sentence anymore when you text or email people. You can simply send them a ☺ and they will know that all is well.

Let's take a look at the definition of an emoji, according to Dictonary. com: "A small digital picture or pictorial symbol that represents a thing, feeling, concept, etc." Actually, I am amazed to see this after years of trying to teach my healing students how to use symbols. Now they've become a truly integral part of our culture.

I laugh at some of the new images they keep coming out with because I'll be busy sending a text and a little photo will pop up which is so accurate and cute! My only fear, in terms of language, is that eventually with so many symbols and fewer words, we may forget how to write, spell, and construct a full sentence! For example, I recently heard on the news that a high school has decided to translate one of

Shakespeare's classics into emojis. Seriously? I think that's a bit much, don't you? Then again, long before the emoji was around, people used symbols in ancient civilizations such as Egypt to communicate with each other, and we have architectural evidence of how brilliant they were, so perhaps this new increase in symbols is a good thing.

In modern healing techniques, symbols are used to easily convey healing vibrations to self and others. All you have to do is visualize the symbol in your mind's eye, see a drawing of it, or write it out yourself. By so doing, you send a signal to your subconscious mind that represents the full expression of the particular thought being conveyed, and when you're sending that thought through healing, it is successfully transferred to the recipient. It is a far more kinesthetic form of communicating and helps get us in touch with feelings and whole concepts in combination.

Reiki and Healing Symbols

Most healing modalities have symbols that are used to convey the healing intention being sent to the recipient. Reiki is a good example. It would be safe to say that most of my students are Reiki practitioners, and those who aren't have at some time or another received a Reiki healing.

The Japanese healing modality Reiki was developed by Mikao Usui, who ascended Mount Kurama–yama near Kyoto, Japan, for twenty–one days, and during that time, developed Reiki after several healing symbols were downloaded into his third eye. The symbols were pictorial representations of healing intentions, and once he came back from his seclusion to rejoin humanity, he began to teach what he learned. Each of the illuminated symbols represented a powerful healing energy.

As we've been discussing during the course of this book, most healing systems these days are divided into body, mind, and spirit sections. Reiki is no exception.

Reiki practitioners receive attunements into the three levels. Source gives us a wonderful description of what an attunement is like:

> . . . being gentle when harshness is manifested, makes for that attunement to the influences within the soul as well as in the ex-

perience of an entity in material activity, of harmony and peace
and quiet.   1397-1

When you learn Reiki, in the first level you receive your attunement
and begin to open up to the universal life-force. You understand how
energy can flow from Source through your body and hands into another person. Level One is to bring balance and peace to the physical body
and to begin to open you up to higher mental and spiritual realms.

In Reiki Level Two, you are initiated and attuned into the three
symbols which are aligned with the material, mental, and spiritual
aspects of the energy field discussed earlier. The first Reiki symbol
enlivens the physical body and energizes the space you're in, allowing
energy to flow more readily in either the space in the material world,
or within the physical body by moving stagnant energy and making
way for higher vibrations to enter. The second Reiki symbol removes
unwanted blockages and karmic holograms from the past and unwanted emotions from the mental body. The third Reiki symbol has more of
a spiritual nature and works to break up soul patterns and long-term
karmic issues. This symbol also opens passageways in the universe by
enabling you to send your healing Reiki energy over long distances for
the benefit of others.

The formation of Reiki and the three-level system is a great introduction to what we're going to look at later.

I was inspired to write this book after discovering a passage in the life
readings containing seven amazing symbols that Source gave as part of
the initiation process during the Egyptian times of Ra-Ta. Later in the
book I'll share the seven symbols and show you a method we can use
to assist you in bringing balance to your material body, mind, and spirit.

First, let's go ahead and take a look at the incredible readings about
temple life during the times in Egypt, shortly after the fall of Atlantis.

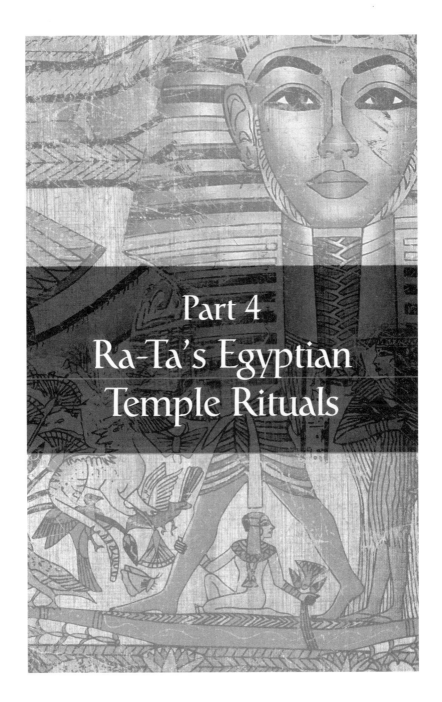

Part 4
Ra-Ta's Egyptian
Temple Rituals

GC: You will have before you the Glad Helpers, members of which are present here, and their study and work in relation to spiritual healing. First you will give six affirmations to be sent those on our prayer list. Then you will have before you the Temple Beautiful in Egypt at about the period 10,500 B.C. after the return of the High Priest RA-TA from banishment. You will describe in detail this temple and the services held in it, explaining how an understanding of the work carried on there may be of help to us now in carrying forward our healing study and work. You will answer the questions.

EC: Yes, we have the group as gathered here, as a group and as individuals, and the work of the Glad Helpers.   281-25

Now, I'd like to formally introduce you to what I call the Edgar Cayce's Egyptian Energy Healing, which I will refer to as ECEEH; but first, let's take a look at the origins of this information.

For me, there is no doubt that I have lived a past life or two, or three, in ancient Egypt, because I had such a strong reaction to Egypt when I first visited there in 2000. At the time, I was only just beginning my spiritual journey and I did not really consciously understand what was happening to me when I began having such an abreaction to Cairo, in particular. Each night I was there, I tossed and turned and had horrible nightmares about wailing people and the building of the Pyramids.

A few years ago, after having additional strange experiences and interviewing others, I finally realized that, although I have been guiding people into past lives via hypnosis for many years now, undergoing a trance is not always necessary to recall past lives. I am now convinced that those dreams I had in Cairo were part of one of my many past-life experiences that I spontaneously recalled by simply going to Egypt.

I have since interviewed hundreds of people and collected incredible case studies about how we can easily slip into spontaneous past-life memories—a phenomenon I call *supretrovie,* or supernatural past-life memory.

The late, great Carl Jung cited a phenomenon called *anamnesis,* which is the soul's knowing of who and what it was in prior lifetimes. Jung believed the soul did indeed know where it had been before in the past, even if those knowings were quiet pangs of intuition bubbling up from the deepest recesses of our subconscious minds.

There is no doubt that when I first explored the life readings concerning the Temple Beautiful and the Temple of Sacrifice, which you're about to see, I felt a knowing that this was truth and that I was either there myself during these times or I knew of them by simply being in that area during later periods. I also believe that all the many souls drawn to the Cayce material are of some kindred and collective consciousness and that there is a very good chance we've been together before.

On July 17, 1935, Cayce gave a critically important reading (281-25) to fourteen members of a group of energy healers called the Glad Helpers. One of those members was Hugh Lynn Cayce. Interestingly, Source gave a similar message to the Glad Helpers when they came to inquire about the Egyptian temples:

> . . . Many of you here were both in and of the temple service, whether in the purifications in the Temple of Sacrifice or the Temple Beautiful . . .   281-25

It is not surprising that the people who want to know about how to use this information to enhance their current lives and help their fellow beings were individuals who had lived during that time in and around 10,500 BC when Ra-Ta was in Egypt. Today, there is still a Glad Helpers group that meets at the A.R.E. Headquarters in Virginia Beach. Could they, too, be connected to these early times?

I have always believed that our souls come back into worldly existence with inklings of who we were before, yet when we incarnate, we agree to dip into what the ancient Greeks call Lethe, the river of forgetfulness. We spend our lifetimes attempting to remember who we are and trying to find the divinity within.

Additionally, I have also long believed that everyone who is attracted to the Cayce material likely connects to the energy from a place and time long ago, either in Egypt, Atlantis, or in the earliest times in Lemuria, when life was non-physical and beings were nothing more than a thought form.

There aren't any coincidences in this life. You and I both know that. There's a reason why you're reading this book right now, and I would venture to guess there is a past-life connection there, just as there was for the Glad Helpers. It's noble to want to recall our past strengths in order to help mankind. The Glad Helpers earnestly sought to hear what they did then and how it might best be used in the present.

This makes complete sense to me. I truly believe that we spend much of our lifetime trying to piece together aspects of ourselves leftover from past incarnations. Why else would this group of healers be so attracted to learn more about the times of Ra-Ta if they weren't there themselves?

I had a similar experience several years ago when I traveled to India for the first time. I was at a conference presenting my research into parallel universes and the fact that I believed beyond a shadow of a doubt that we could create our destinies simply through our thinking.

When I arrived in New Delhi, I was drawn to go have a Naadi Leaf reading, and I went with some friends from the conference. The Naadi Leaves are ancient messages transcribed on bamboo and kept in a sort of hall of records to be consulted by future generations. Written in the now dead language of Tamil, supposedly they were the written accounts of all the people who lived 2000 years ago in a remote village in the south of India.

When I went for the reading, it was so obscure; they did not want you to tell them anything about yourself, not even your name. Your only form of identification was to put your two thumbprints into their little pad of paper kept on the reception desk. Then you took a seat and waited.

When they called me in, they began reading from the books of records, going through a process of narrowing down the documents until they found the one that was about me. How did I know they were speaking to me? They knew things about me—my profession, the real name of my mother who actually uses her middle name, things about my brother, and most telling, the man who spoke no English and actually used a translator to relay his details, actually pronounced my dad's name! They also pinpointed the day of the week on which I was born and began pointing out some of the highlights of my life and what was to come. All of this with nothing more than a thumbprint!

This experience sent me into a spiritual tailspin that has literally taken me years to resolve, because how could I believe in our complete ability to create reality when these known facts were so readily available? I've since come to believe that destiny is a mix of preplanned moments combined with the creative and dynamic force of free will. Somewhere between the two we shape our destinies.

Having my leaves read reminds me a lot of the reading Source gave to the Glad Helpers because when I went to have this done, the five other women who were with me all had leaves there too, and we were fast friends who were apparently some kind of soul group that had come together during this time in India.

I told the ladies I believed that we were the scribes who wrote down those messages thousands of years ago. We wrote those messages to ourselves, and after having the leaf readers tell me that I was to arrive at their offices at a certain age (yes, they knew my age and I gave them no birth details about myself), then there was no doubt in my mind that we reincarnated and decided as a soul group to get together and meet at that specific place and time to share the experience together and to reconnect after a long separation. The experience was profound, to say the least, and one I will never forget as long as I live. The reality of knowing we had been there before could not be denied.

Truth is important in all things. Yet truth is not always true. People can believe something and have it scientifically invalidated at any moment. When I returned to the conference in New Delhi, many believed we were taken in by charlatans, while others were simply fascinated because people who had lived in India their whole lives and had heard about the leaf readings said there were only a certain number of people alive who actually had leaves. Many of the people who went seeking Naadi Leaf readings were sent away empty-handed because they had no leaves in the archives to read.

What I will tell you is that I always give you my truth, as I see it. Because I believe strongly in the multiverse, I know that different realities exist simultaneously in the unified field. It is possible that the influxes and insights of intuitive information floating in from the divine and the destinies that play out are impulses coming from different realities overlapping on themselves and affecting us in various ways.

I definitely believe I've lived in India in many lifetimes, and I believe what the Cayce life readings and Source tell us—that Egypt began 10,500 years ago, or more. I believe that as surely as I believe my own name. Many mainstream scientists are on board with that fact as well, and others aren't there yet in terms of being able to grapple with the reality that life as we know it and the mainstream belief systems we've become so indoctrinated in believing are not representational of actual reality and the true timeline for our planet.

If you are attracted to the study of this material, draw on the truth or the resonance within your own soul. You may find this information, I hope, to be as important and transformational as I've found it to be over the years. If it feels real to you, then it's real. If not, then perhaps you will find the study fascinating for other reasons, but just know that yes, I'm a believer. Big time.

So, let's dive into this fascinating material. This next section will break down the Glad Helper's reading by Cayce to give you a clearer understanding of the healing work done in the ancient Egyptian times in a step-by-step format that we can benefit from today.

Description of the Temple

In structure, this: There had been gathered from all the nations of the earth that which represented from their environ, their surrounding, the most beautiful gift; that it might be a reminder of those, to those, that purified or gave themselves in service or activity there, of the beauty of service of EVERY land in this preparation of the bodies for their greater service and for their intermingling with those of the earth's environ as well as enabling the servants, the workers, the priestess, the prophetess, those that labored—or joyously gave themselves—to give their activity for others.

The materials outwardly were of the mountains nigh unto the upper waters of the Nile.

It was in the form of the pyramid, within which was the globe—which represented to those who served there a service to the world.

The furnishings may be surmised from the fact that the most beautiful things from each land were gathered there; gold, silver, onyx, iron, brass, silk, satins, linen.   281-25

The Glad Helpers wanted to know what the temple was like, and Cayce told them in great detail. Source also gave readings to others with descriptions of aura charts that described how the Temple looked and how they might recreate the scene to aid them in their current lives:

Above this put an INSIDE view of the Temple Beautiful; this indicating the seven stations, or seven centers, and with figures at each station. This would be very elaborate as to color tones; being as of an opalescence hue, with the heavens seen in the dome or ceiling—and these would be indicated over the various stations—the sun, the moon, the cross (the southern cross indicated here), the dippers, and the two large stars indicating the morning and the evening star, as well as the dog star. The cross—put this as a square, or each of the same length lines, over the central figure, or the figure indicated as being opposite the sun. The dress of the figures should indicate the colors of the rainbow, or the seven primary colors; these carrying, then, the indication of attainment of the entity through the experience in that particular period of unfoldment.   993-6

While we cannot hope to completely recreate what was done in those early times, after researching the readings and other sources, I believe this will be the closest we are ever going to get to relive the practices of Ra–Ta and his followers in 10,500 BC. One of the other major aspects of temple life was music, which we will look at next.

Music

Music was an important part of life in the Temple, but not simply for entertainment purposes. Several people who had life readings served as musicians during this special time in history. To be selected as musicians, people would have to be a highly advanced, highly skilled practitioners who had worked on themselves and maintained a proper frequency and intention balance throughout their sojourn on earth. Here are a few interesting life readings for some of the most talented among the musicians.

One woman discovered she was a music teacher in her current life and apparently brought that latent talent through with her to the present incarnation:

> The entity then, as a daughter of the Priest in those periods when there were greater activities of a spiritual nature, supplied the music that would span the distances between loneliness and crowds, that would make for the lifting of the soul in those periods even when operations were performed under the soothing strains of same. The entity perfected the stringed instruments. And when there was the roll of the organ in the ecstasies reached in the Temple Beautiful, again the entity supplied same.
>
> Thus in music may the entity again unfold to that ability to away those in distress, those that are fearful, those that are doubtful; as well as bringing those that are beset with doubts to the joyousness of a walk in the garden with Jesus.
>
> Make that the theme of thine own song, make it the theme of thine own preparation of music; for it will raise thee, too, to that experience as ye found in that Egyptian environ, with the Priest as well as the saints in the Temple Beautiful and the activities thereabout.   3234-1

Another person was a musical conductor in Egypt:

> Before that we find the entity was in the Egyptian land when there were those activities with the Priest Ra-Ta. The entity was among the daughters of Ra-Ta, active in the developing of the songs in the periods of activities in the Temple Beautiful. The entity then was a musician upon the lyre as well as the conductor of the music in the temple worship, as well as that to arouse the activities of the peoples. In the name then Ineul-Ian.   5262-1

A housewife learned the following about her past life in Temple service:

> The entity then acted in these capacities, then, of enabling those to be brought from the peoples or groups that labored to pass through the purges in the Temple of Sacrifice; arising to the musician in the Temple Beautiful, seeing the performing of the regenerating of hopes, desires and purposes in the minds and bodies of individuals that were aroused to such activity by the experience of the entity in the later experience on the day of Pentecost.
> In the Temple Beautiful the entity developed, for it became not only the scribe but the musician for those activities through that experience.   2581-2

Each of these readings demonstrates the importance music plays in reshaping lives.

Toning with Sound

> In the activities then, there were first the songs, the music, as we have indicated that YE sing: Ar-r-r—Ou-u—Ur-r [Har-rrr-rr-aum says Dr. I. C. Sharma]; which makes for the losing of even the association of the body with that save the VIBRATIONS of which the body was then composed; yea now is, though encased in a much more hardened matter, as to materiality; which made for the vibrating of same with light, that BECOMES color, that becomes tone, that becomes activity.   281-25

Toning with sound by singing musical notes to shift energies within and without the body was another important aspect of working with music in the Egyptian Temple.

Source describes the reality that music is a key to loosening up stuck patterns in our bodies. Music gets us moving and shifts vibrations. Clearly, this fact was not only known but also used in the earliest of times.

Cayce also describes the correlation between the notes and colors within the energy bodies. He stated that by playing certain tones, you can actually loosen material reality and raise frequencies to create energy of a higher nature.

Years ago, I experimented quite a bit with sound toning by singing various notes as I was guided. This is an incredibly powerful process, and as usual, Source is correct that nothing will loosen up the bonds of material reality faster than music.

Even in our mainstream lives, you are likely affected by music. Haven't you heard a song you love and been instantly lifted into a brighter mood? Likewise, music can evoke powerful memories stored in our holographic bodies. You've likely heard a song and been whisked back to a time long ago with memories so fresh that the events connected to them feel as though they are happening at that very moment.

Throughout the ages, most indigenous cultures have music as part of their ritual practice. Luckily for us, Cayce tells what the participants should be singing and toning:

> Seek then IN tone, all of you: Ar-r-r-r-r-AR [Har-rrrrr-aum says Dr. I. C. Sharma]; that ye may know how the emanations, that are termed as the colors of the body, make for the expression then given.   281-25

Later, the Glad Helpers had a follow-up reading and asked exactly how this should sound:

> (Q) In the reading on the Temple Beautiful, July 17, 1935 [281-25], in Par. 23, where it says, "Seek, then, in tone, all of you, A-r-r-r-r-r-ar," please give what key it is sung in.
> (A) It is the COMBINATION, or a treble from C to C. 281-26

The Glad Helpers were not the only people to receive detailed information about the toning in the temple. Another woman received a reading and was told that she, too, served as a valuable asset in the times of the Temple Beautiful and was skilled in the methods:

> . . . Turn for the moment, then, to thy service in the Temple Beautiful. Here we have those incantations that are as but the glorifying of constructive forces in all of their activity within the

human emotions that may be known in the present day; for glory, not of self, not of the ability of self, but the glory of the oneness of purpose, of the I AM of the individual for the glorifying of that creative energy within self that may keep the whole body, whole body-individual, whole body as of the group, the whole body as of those within the sound as it ranges from the highest to the lowest of the incantations within; following that known in thine own present as i-e-o-u-e-i-o-umh. [?Ar-e-o-u-ummm?] [Har-rrrrr-aum says Dr. I. C. Sharma.]

These as they make for the raising of that from within of the Creative Forces, as it arises along that which is set within the inner man as that cord of life that once severed may separate, does separate, that balance between the mind, the body, the soul; these three, as accorded within the human forces, are the activities that were carried on by thyself in movement of body in its EVERY motion that made for the lifting up, the intoning in of self within . . .

                                                                275-43

We can attune to these tones and raise our vibrations by simply humming along with the notes. Since Source says these are all notes between treble C and C, I am reminded of the holiday classic *The Sound of Music* and the song *Do-Re-Mi*, which is basically an exercise to sing up the musical scale. Try singing that or humming it, and I think you'll be fairly close to what Cayce and Source are talking about here.

If you don't have a piano, any instrument will do, or these days, I've worked quite a bit with Garage Band on my iPhone which is an amazing example of how technology can benefit us. You can pull a tiny keyboard up and start playing and singing along. Incredible!

Attuning Auras and Colors

The entity then arose in power, in authority among men in the Temple of Sacrifice FIRST, and then in the Temple of Beauty— the Temple Beautiful.

For there the entity gained the abilities to make for the harmonizing colors to those extents wherein each individual was and is as yet clothed with ITS individual color—as ye call aura. 1436-2

The concept and importance of auras and color in the Cayce readings cannot be understated. The life readings are filled with discussions about the importance of recognizing and working with the aura—the colored energy field that exists around the physical body discussed earlier in the book. Vibrations translate to musical notes on the scale and colors in the rainbow spectrum. When you're off, simply attune yourself, or retune yourself to the proper notes and soon you will achieve balance in the body.

In the Egyptian times, music was used to attune the colors within the physical body, so they properly aligned with the notes in the musical scale. Some individuals who received readings from Cayce were told that helping others align themselves was their duty.

As souls, we likely had incredible gifts and talents that we no longer remember how to use. Seeing the aura and attuning ourselves to a state of peace and perfection was one of our special abilities. The good news is that as we progress in our spiritual work, we can remember those long–forgotten aspects of ourselves and create greater peace and harmony in our lives.

Earlier we talked about chakras and how they represent colors within our bodies. How do we work with our chakras to bring them into alignment? It's done by envisioning the ideal, as Cayce mentioned, and imagining each energy center fully open, functioning and vibrating at the appropriate color within the rainbow spectrum.

Let's do a quick exercise to do just that. Ready?

Exercise

Sit in a comfortable chair with your hands in your lap and your feet on the floor. Breathe in light, healing, and peace. Exhale any concerns and tensions. Good job.

Now imagine that a bright red ball of light is traveling down through the top of your head, moving through your spine, and landing at the base of your spine. Feel the ball of light as it swirls around. Imagine it is bright and full and vibrant. Allow that red light to open your root chakra and notice feeling grounded to the earth. If you would like, you can imagine a C note as you perceive the color red.

Next, imagine that a bright orange ball of light is traveling down through the top of your head, moving through your spine and landing a couple of inches below your navel. Feel the ball of light as it swirls around. Imagine it is bright orange, full and vibrant. Allow that orange light to open your sacral chakra and notice feeling new creative energies awaken. If you would like, you can imagine a D note as you perceive the color orange.

Next, imagine that a bright yellow ball of light travels down through the top of your head, moves through your spine, and lands in the area of your solar plexus near the intersection of your ribs. Feel the ball of light as it swirls around. Imagine it is bright yellow, full and vibrant. Allow that yellow light to open your solar plexus chakra, giving you new strength and courage. If you would like, you can imagine an E note as you perceive the color yellow.

Next, imagine that a bright green ball of light travels down through the top of your head, moving through your spine and landing in the area of your heart chakra. Feel the ball of light as it swirls around your heart, opening you, relaxing you. Imagine it is bright green, full and vibrant. Allow that green ball of light to open your heart chakra, giving you amazing health and feelings of love for yourself and others. If you would like, you can imagine an F note as you notice the color green.

Next, imagine that a bright blue ball of light travels down through the top of your head and lands in the area of your throat chakra, just above your collar bone. Feel the ball of light as it swirls around in your throat. Imagine it is bright blue, full and vibrant. Allow that blue light to open your throat chakra, giving you clarity in all your communications. If you would like, you can imagine a G note as you notice the color blue.

Next, imagine that a bright purple ball of light travels down through the top of your head, and lands in the area of your third eye in the center of your forehead. Feel the ball of light as it swirls around your forehead, opening you, relaxing you. Imagine it is bright purple, full and vibrant. Allow that purple ball of light to open your third eye chakra, expanding your intuition and giving you insights into the inner workings of yourself and others. If you would like, you can imagine an A note as you notice the color purple.

Finally, imagine you feel an amazing ball of white light that pours in through the top of your head, opening your crown chakra. Allow this white healing light to spin above and within your head and mind, opening you up to Spirit, opening your crown chakra center, connecting you with your Higher Power and all sentient beings. If you would like, you can imagine a B note as you notice the color white.

Now that all of the vibrant balls of healing colored light are in place, imagine they are all full and illuminated, balanced and open. Allow them to be equally opened and all centers to be in total alignment now.

When you are ready, open your eyes. Three, two, one, you're back, feeling more balanced and refreshed than you did before.

How was that? This is a super simple process you can easily visualize to help balance all of your energy centers from the inside out.

Colored Water

If you prefer a more physical way to balance your chakras and attune your aura and colors, you can drink color-charged water. This is something I go into in great detail during my gem healing courses. Because all color has a unique vibration, you can create "colored water" which is incredibly helpful for bringing balance to the aura.

Here are the steps:

1) Find a glass jar such as one used to make sun tea. The lid can be plastic, but the jar itself should be clear glass for best results.

2) Fill your jar with pure filtered water.

3) Select a piece of translucent colored cellophane. You can find this in wrapping paper sections at your local store. A few examples include:

Red—helps ground you

Orange—stimulates creativity

Yellow—aids digestion and stomach issues

Green—great for heart healing, both physically and emotionally

Blue—helps communication, thyroid, and other throat issues

Purple—opens the third eye and develops psychic awareness

4) Wrap your chosen colored cellophane around your glass jar and fasten it with a twist tie or tape so that the wrap stays secure on the jar.

5) Place the jar outside in the sun and allow the life-force of the sun to heat up the water.

6) Keep it outside for a minimum of twenty minutes to a maximum of overnight.

7) Bring the water inside and enjoy your colored water.

The other way to get the same results would be to use a colored glass bottle such as bright blue or red, although colored bottles are not always easy to come by, so use whatever you find.

The colored water is a version of the gem elixir process I talk about in my gem healing books. When you soak the water in the colored vibrations given off by this wrap, the water actually changes and will taste different from when you first put the filtered water into your jar. Try an experiment and compare red water with green water. They will taste different. That just proves that colors really have unique vibrations and when you drink the water, the molecules go into the body and shift your vibrations so that you soak in the desired color.

With gemstones, you could do the same except that many minerals are too fragile to soak, so with that process, I recommend using only a clear quartz crystal. This might explain why the cellophane works so well on the bottles.

Theoretically you want to balance all the chakra centers evenly though, so many times you would use only the colored–water process if you were attempting to rectify an imbalance. Try the water though. It's an interesting process and quite fun.

Next, we will take a look at the ways the ancient ones got these energy centers moving in the right direction—with dance.

Dance

> Before that the entity was in the Egyptian land, in the activities of the Temple Beautiful when there were those influences wrought for the body-development—the entity being the activity leader especially in the dance, the rhythmic dance . . .   2247-1

The life readings describe many people who served as dancers in the healing temples. Sounds fun, right? I don't think we typically see the importance of how dance can heal, but in fact, it does as Source describes in greater detail here:

> The entity then was among those that supplied music in the Temple Beautiful, as well as in the dance—or in the activities of the body to bring to the consciousness of individuals the change being wrought in the mental being, as physical change was wrought in the body, during temple service   314-1

Dancing was a huge part of temple life, according to Cayce. Again, as with the music, dancing enabled the physical body to loosen and separate itself from material reality in order to raise frequencies and attain the higher vibrations of the spirit.

Not until recently was I again reminded how healing dancing can be. After years of forsaking my former exercise classes at my gym for swimming, I was guided that it was time to make a change. In hindsight, I can see it was likely in part due to the fact I would be writing this book. I noticed there were some amazing Zumba teachers with huge class sizes, and I decided to go ahead and take classes from all the instructors.

Zumba is a fitness class that utilizes core dance moves from salsa and other methods, yet it is designed with fitness in mind and is known to burn a ton of calories. One of the great things about Zumba is the music. The eclectic mix of Latin, hip-hop, and Indian makes it a multicultural event that is incredibly fun.

People from all walks of life can get together and have a great time. When people are dancing and connecting to the universal rhythms of primal beats, it is amazing how well everyone gets along. A little more dancing, a little less talking would perhaps be a great formula for society in general.

What is interesting to watch are the stomping feet, clapping hands, and the ability of everybody to get in tune with each other's energy. It is absolutely amazing. When I hear certain tribal beats, I can't help but think that the group is collectively tuning into not only their own potential past-life experiences but also to a collective consciousness of the ancestors from times long past.

The other incredible thing that I have come to truly appreciate about Zumba is the way the teachers always stop in between songs and ask everyone an important question that is too often missed in today's busy world: "How are you feeling?" Feelings are important. Jumping up and down, singing, dancing, and having fun are sure to make you feel better than you did when you arrived.

Therefore, it's not surprising to imagine Source reminding us that by dancing, we loosen up our physical selves, and as a result, good things as well as powerful energetic shifts are bound to happen. Dance is an incredible gift for shifting our frequencies for the better.

Initiation

Then there was the giving by the Prophetess of the seal of life that was set upon each and every one who passed through these experiences, how or in what field of activity the relationships were of an individual to its fellow man in maintaining material existence; being in the world yet not OF the world.   281-25

Rituals are a major part of spiritual practice, and certainly our souls have participated in a variety of initiations in our past lives when we were part of various sacred communities throughout the ages. Initiations are offered to take us from one state of being into another. As alchemists would say, we transmute the lead of dense materiality into precious gold and rise above the mundane world through the process of initiation by walking through doors and ascending into higher realms. Undergoing a process lets our Higher Selves know that we have crossed a threshold and are imbued with new and powerful information.

I am set on providing you with all you need to do this system for yourself, so you will not be required to attend an expensive class to have an activation or initiation to enjoy the benefits of ECEEH. We will talk more about the initiation in the section on the Cayce healing symbols, and I will show you how to use these symbols to give yourself an initiation into the system.

If and when we meet for an Edgar Cayce Egyptian Healing class sometime in the future, then I'll be happy to initiate you, but for now, for the sake of practicality, the power will be in your hands.

Journey to the Temple

Ye ask, where is this now? Disintegrated and in that sphere ye may enter, and some have entered, where these are sealed as with the seven seals of the law in that these experiences now become as those of thine activities among thy fellow man.   281-25

Here Cayce and Source address the obvious question before it was even asked—Where could we go to experience this Temple in three-dimensional reality? Apparently, we cannot because according to Cayce, the Temple no longer exists in our world, and yet Source suggests we may be able to better access the Temple via the theater of the mind, using the power of imagination.

This has been one of the fundamental principles in my work as a hypnotherapist—to get people to loosen ties with material waking reality and trust in the imaginative forces in consciousness so they can travel back and forth in time to receive healing, insights, and information. We mentioned past-life connections to Egypt before, and this next exercise will help you uncover some of those ties.

Cayce paints a vivid picture of the Temple when he sums up the atmosphere in the following reading in such a way that it may trigger memories for those who may have been there in the past:

> THESE then, made for that as ye have in thine experiences in the present expressed: First in cleanliness, in purifying of the body, in the washing in blood, in water, that ye may be purified before thyself first and then before others. The anointing with the incense, making for the raising of that ye know as thine senses or perception or consciousness of the activities to all the faults, by comparison, as arose among others.
>
> From those activities ye have that first as thine service of preparation, of birth, of consecration, of purification, of those things that later become the hospitalization, the care of the ill in body, in mind; the divinations of those tempted from within and those tempted from without. Little study is made in the present of this phase of man's experience.
>
> The teaching, the preparation, the ministering, the song, the music, the activities that give expression, arise in man's experience from those activities in the Temple Beautiful.   281-25

You can easily travel to this sacred space in the Egyptian Temple by simply going on a journey. Let's do that now.

Exercise

Sit or recline in a comfortable chair with your hands in your lap and close your eyes. Breathe in peace, healing, and relaxation, and exhale tension. Very good.

I want you to imagine there is a beam of pure white light coming down in through the top of your head. Feel this light as it moves down through your forehead, into your eyes, your nose, your mouth, into your neck and shoulders, your arms, elbows, wrists, hands, fingertips.

That healing light is continuing to travel down your spine into your heart and lungs. Breathe in the high vibrational healing light and feel the loving energy as it continues down to the base of your spine and moves into your legs and flows down and out the soles of your feet.

Allow the light to become stronger now and notice it is creating a beautiful golden ball of light that surrounds you by about three feet in all directions. Feel yourself floating inside this golden ball of light and know that within that golden ball of light only that which is of your highest good can come through.

Imagine up ahead there is a doorway in front of you. Go ahead and walk or float up toward the door and you will notice you are in front of the Egyptian Temple.

Notice the sign above the doorway which reads:

LORD, LEAD THOU THE WAY. I COMMIT MY BODY, MY MIND, TO BE ONE WITH THEE . . .   281-25

In a moment, when I count down from three, you will enter the Temple and notice what you notice. Ready? Three, two, one . . . walk through the door now. Be there now and notice what's happening.

What do you see?

How do you feel?

Are you alone or with other people? If you are with others, is there anyone there whom you recognize from your current life? If so, who?

Take your time to enjoy all there is to offer. As you start to look around, you are approached by Ra-Ta, the Priest.

Imagine you can speak to Ra-Ta about your soul, and your soul's development. Imagine you can ask him about your soul's journey.

What is your soul's purpose? How are you working on developing your purpose in your current life?

Were you in Egypt in the past? If so, what was your role in society? Imagine this information is easy to discover.

Ask Ra-Ta to tell you anything else you need to know that would be for your highest good at this time.

What does he tell you?

Take a moment and feel the vibrational energy of this sacred space. How does it make you feel?

What sounds do you hear?

What learning can you bring from this space into your current life?

When you're finished, imagine you can thank Ra-Ta for working with you today.

Go ahead, turn around, and walk back toward the entrance you came from and step back out to where we started.

Notice now how much lighter and brighter you feel as a result of this journey. Know you can come back here again for further insights into your soul development. Good job!

In a moment, when I count back from five, you will come back into the room, feeling awake, refreshed and better than you did before. Five, you are grounded, centered, and balanced. Four, bring this knowledge and information with you to benefit you in your current life; three, know that you are surrounded by a protective healing light always; two, grounded, centered, and balanced; and one, you're back!

How was that? Did you receive any surprising information? What about initiations or information you can use to assist you in your current life?

You may want to make a few notes on the journey so you can refer to them later, and of course, you can always travel to the Temple again to learn more later.

How to Use This Information in the Present

Then, in using and in applying and associating same with thine activities in that experience, and that manner in which ye may use same in the present:

So attune thyselves that ye may harken, not as to an experience only; but rather LIVE and BE the experience in the hearts of those that are seeking to find their way; whether in the troubles of the body, of the mind, or whether they are lost among those turmoils of the cry, "This way—That way"—Here and there. Be the experience to someone to light their lives, their bodies, their minds to thy LIVING Lord, thy brother, the Christ! For He has promised in His words in thine own heart, that keeps the hope, that keeps the fires of thine own heart aflame, "Ye finding me may know the JOY of the Lord."   281-25

The Glad Helpers were earnest seekers wanting to be able to actually use the information they received from Cayce and Source to aid their fellow man—a noble aspiration. Source sums up the highest ideal for any of us to follow: to simply be there for people when they are confused and hold space and light for them. A beautiful gesture.

That's really what any energy healing is about: holding space, seeing people who may not currently be at their best, moving past current troubles to attain higher ground and happiness.

He also reminded everyone in the Glad Helper's group again of the fact they had been in the Temple service in past lives:

> As many of you served there, as many experienced those purifications for an active service among their fellow man in an INDIVIDUAL experience, so may ye purify thy minds and thy bodies, or purify thy BODIES that thy MIND may put ON Christ, the garments of a living Lord, that ye may be not as ones stumbling, as ones fearful of this or that, but SURE and CERTAIN in the joys of a risen Lord; that indeed thy body in its expressions may be the Temple BEAUTIFUL for thy LIVING Lord.   281-25

Now that we've explored the Temple, I will share detailed step-by-step information in this section on how I began using this information. Then I will disclose my findings from a group who has agreed to receive extended sessions with this modality. In the final section I will show you how to apply what we've discussed so you can easily do this to aid yourself and others. In this section, we will do some exercises that will directly benefit our material body, mind, and spirit.

Removing Unwanted Influences from Body, Mind, and Spirit

> Before that the entity was in the Egyptian land during those periods when there were the preparations of individuals for activities through the offices of the Temple of Sacrifice and the Temple Beautiful. The entity there began its first activities in aiding in the Temple of Sacrifice, being an administrator of the antidotes when there were those applications of what ye in the present call surgery.   4016-1

One of the important aspects to the way the Egyptian Temple Healings were conducted is that initiates had to first go to the Temple of Sacrifice to remove unwanted influences and cleanse themselves before they could ascend to the Temple Beautiful.

Recently, I was teaching my full-day gem workshop, and one of the attendees asked about this very concept. I have always believed and experienced the fact that it is necessary to remove unwanted influences first and then replace those energies with higher ideals and frequencies. There are two reasons for this. First, you want your space to be clear and clean, so to speak, before doing your work for others; and second, you must be as clear a channel as you can be before offering your services to others. When doing any kind of energy healing, you can't possibly expect to help others if you haven't helped yourself first. It's like the old saying on the airplane that if the oxygen masks drop from the ceiling during flight, you need to put the mask on yourself first, otherwise you can't be of service to others. And when you do serve, you want everyone to receive your best by being the best you can be.

In this section, we will do some clearing processes to create the space needed to work with some healing symbols Cayce mentions in the life readings.

Purifying Body, Mind, and Spirit

First in the Temple of Sacrifice it became necessary, as indicated, for the signifying of the individual's desire, by its activity of purifying of self through those days of purification—that later became exemplified in many of the forms of religious ceremony of purifying and preparation that there might be put away from the body and from the mind those things that would lead or direct or tend to make for the associations with the old self.   264-50

The life readings describe in detail how the aspirants were prepared to receive initiations by going through various rituals in the Temple of Sacrifice. In this section, we will look at several of these clearing processes and discuss how we can bring these ancient methods into modern times to aid in our own self-development and healing.

In order to achieve healing and rid the self of old, outdated patterns, rituals would need to be performed for quieting the mind and raising the frequencies. One woman who played an important role in the healing temples was given detailed information on how she successfully achieved purification during her past life in Egypt:

> These in the activities of the Temple of Sacrifice were removed first by the mental, the physical dedicating of the self to an individual purpose; that of enabling others, of bringing to others that necessary and the necessity of the purifying of body, the purifying of mind, the purifying of intent, the dedicating of purpose, the dedicating of activity for the pure relationships with activities among those that had dedicated their lives to an activity that would present the body as a channel, a means, a manner, a way of being not only as represented in the Temple Beautiful as a BODY-beautiful but as a service also—of every nature, of every character.   264-50

Let's break down the steps listed above:

1) Purify the Body
There are many ways to purify the body, and several readings allude to our food as being a way to achieve a balanced body.

2) Purify the Mind
Thinking positive thoughts, connecting with Christ–Consciousness, and ridding the subconscious of lower frequency thinking to achieve a state of unconditional love for all are the goals for this directive.

3) Purify the Intent
This section asks us to answer the ever–elusive question—What do we want to create?

4) Dedicating Ourselves to Our Purpose through Activity
Not only must we dedicate ourselves to our mission on earth, but that purpose must be aligned with the highest good or spiritual ideals that are of benefit to our fellow man. In addition, we must actually take action to achieve something of worth.

In aligning with what we discussed in the last section about the three spiritual bodies, nearly all energy healing modalities that have become popular in the past hundred years follow a three–part system to address the material or physical body, the mental body, and the spiritual body. In each level, clearings occur, energy is shifted, frequencies are raised, and each step serves as a building block upon the others. You begin with the body and graduate to the higher levels of mind and spirit once certain tasks are completed.

In the times of Ra–Ta, people would go through several processes in order to achieve the highest levels of initiations. The Temple of Sacrifice was dedicated to the purification of the body, and once that had been achieved, aspirants would graduate to the higher levels.

Let's take a look at some of the purification processes and tools Cayce discussed that we can use for our bodies and see how we can apply them to our own lives today.

Part 1: Material/Body

Fire

> Then came the periods of passing through the testings that were set as near as possible to the fires of nature, that there might be the emptying as through those experiences that had made for those very influences that brought about the lower forces in the experience of the body.   264-50

The same woman mentioned earlier received a detailed reading listing the various stages of the cleansing process. In the reading, Source seems to imply that participants were actually introduced to a real fire that burned off their unwanted influences. We can only imagine what this might have been like!

Modern seekers participate in the fire-walking rituals offered by various motivational speakers where they are taken into a deep trance and asked to ascend into a higher realm of consciousness such that when they walk across the coals, they do not burn their feet. I've never done a fire walk, but I know plenty of people who have crossed the burning coals. Apparently, this is easily done by most people as long as they walk steadily and slowly and do not linger too long on the coals. I'm inclined to believe Source is speaking about a similar ritual here.

Since we obviously don't want to go to such extremes to experience the healing purifications of fire, here are some alternative ways you can use this transformational element:

Candle Lighting

Set up candles in your sacred space and ask that the flames transform energies around you and your healing space so that they may be of the highest vibrational frequency.

Burning Ritual

You can use a fire that is preferably in an outdoor place such as a fire pit. I like to use my little chiminea for burning rituals.

There are two ways to do this:

1) Letting Go and Releasing—Write down on paper things you want to let go of and burn the paper in the open flames. For example, if you wish to release fear or things from the past, write them down and watch them burn, transforming into nothingness before your eyes. Imagine you can feel the release of these energies and the new space created by letting go.

Source cited this kind of releasing in the following reading:

> Hence the entity also from those periods of its activity rose to that position in the Temple Beautiful service, which was that organ or that body or that place of service and activity in which there were the trainings as it were of the individuals, from the desires of the natures of flesh itself . . .   264-50

2) Creating and Manifesting—Write down goals and intentions and release those to the fires of creation. In a similar fashion to the banishing ritual, here you write instead what you do want, toss that into the flames, and allow the intentions to be consumed by the all-knowing void, letting your detachment to outcome be expressed through the fire. Again, there is a sense of relief and release as the energies are transmuted into the ether.

Source said that the fires created an actual regeneration of the person after such a cleansing:

> . . . purified by the service and activity, through rote—yet the very influences that raised within the bodies that had been brought for purifying the regeneration by the fires of these, by the fires of purification. 264-50

Ideally, such a ritual would do both. First, by burning off the past, space is created for new, higher vibratory energies to come in; and once that process is complete, you can invite what you do want, as Cayce called it the *ideal*, and release your prayers into the void of creation.

Calling in Fire with the Flame Meditation

The other way I frequently use to call in the fire energy is to simply imagine it in my mind. See a flame engulfing your body, washing impurities out of your energy bodies and chakras mentioned earlier. Imagine as the flames move over the body, you rid yourself of lower energies and prepare yourself for higher mastery of whatever it is you are going to undertake.

To accomplish this, you can do the following exercise:

Exercise

Sit or lie down in a comfortable and safe space. Close your eyes and begin to relax. Go ahead and take a deep breath in through your nose, breathing in peace, healing, and relaxation while exhaling tension and concern. With each breath you take, notice you are becoming more and more relaxed.

Now imagine the flames of a fire appear before you. Go ahead and step into those flames. Feel the fire on the soles of your feet. Very good. Notice the flames getting higher and higher as they move up, up, up the body, over the legs—the calves, knees, and thighs. Allow the flames to continue traveling upward to the base of the spine, up your back, through your stomach, burning away any unwanted energies. Imagine this fire relaxes you and heals you as it continues to travel up through the lungs, into the heart, into the shoulders, up, up, up into the neck to the base of the skull, traveling higher and higher into your cheeks, eyes, forehead.

Feel the fire pouring out the crown center of your head, creating a luminous golden light that surrounds your body, encircling you by about three feet in all directions. Very good. Allow this light to raise your vibrations, preparing you for your healing work.

Continue to sit in this light for a few more minutes until you begin to feel a lightening of your energy, a relaxation. When you are ready, you will return to your space feeling clear and energized and better than before. Good job!

How do you feel? Hopefully the process was liberating and yet not quite as dramatic as walking in an actual fire.

Still, thanks to the ability of your imagination, you can achieve incredible results by harnessing the power of your own mind.

Oil

So with this body, passing through those periods; and then the anointing with the oil, the passing through or raising of the vibratory forces within self, the activities and assistance through the priest and the activities that made for the burning of same as it were upon the altars of nature.   264-50

According to the life readings, once the body has been purified by the flames of the fire, oil is used to further anoint the aspirant and prepare the body for the ritual temple work.

Source gives a clue as to which oil might have been used in the times of the Temple Beautiful when a woman asks about a recurring smell:

(Q) Periodically for months I smelled either glycerine or witch-hazel upon awakening. Can I employ either of these gainfully to aid others?

(A) Part of the oils used in temple service, and these are emotions that arise from experiences. These are only signs, not as directions; rather as assurances. Do not use them as directions. Keep them as assurances.   1620-2

Cayce always reminded people not to become too dependent on what he called omens. We should use tools, but not become so attached to them that we cannot function without them. He asks the woman to use the scent as a reminder of times past, but not to use that information as a crutch.

Witch hazel was mentioned in the life readings over a thousand times. Cayce often recommended it as a remedy for circulation issues as in the following:

> For this condition we find that a course of hydrotherapy treatments would be best—which would include first a mild fume bath—using Witchhazel in the fumes . . .   69-5

Glycerin was also mentioned numerous times, many for eliminations, and one interesting reading to help someone's scalp:

> The pure soap, with a little glycerine in the water, would be the best for washing the scalp and hair—or head.   457-3

Interestingly, glycerin is used in many natural essential oil soaps on the market today. Once again, Cayce was ahead of his time. Based on the following, we could conclude that oils can be more spiritual in nature rather than physical:

> (Q) Have I any healing power?
> (A) What power HASN'T the body, with that faith, with that UNDERSTANDING! These may be used in MANY directions by the laying on of hands, and with prayer—anointing as of oil—as has been given, anointing with oil—pouring in of those of the spirit, that knowledge, of understanding—will bring BLESSINGS to many. Do not NEGLECT that that has been committed into thy keeping—thine own!   2112-1

The idea that there were oils used as part of temple rituals is not hard to imagine. Ancient Egyptians were among the first peoples to use oils in rituals, particularly for mummification. Some popular oils in ancient Egypt were:

Cedar

I applied the gasoline, oil of mustard and oil of cedar this morning and there was a relaxation in the lumbar and sacral region that surely surprised me, and I am sure it would have surprised anyone. Thanks to the Lord is my prayer for sending such helpful messages through you. I assure you that I will carry out whatever the readings tell us to do, for they know.   Report 264-13

Ancient Egyptians used cedar oil in embalming practices after realizing it was effective as an insecticide and therefore kept bugs away from the bodies. The Sumerians used cedar in paint. The original variety used by the ancient ones is no longer around as that species of cedar is now extinct. These days, the oil is now called cedarwood. It is considered an antifungal and can be toxic if used in high doses, but as with many of the Cayce recommendations, when used in moderation, the oil has its merits.

Cinnamon

(Q) What causes recurrent sharp pains in lower jaw and front teeth?
(A) As indicated, a psychic experience. Paint same with the Oil of Cinnamon when this occurs. This as we find is not true toothache, but rather the transition of those nerve forces in a developing period for the body.   1206-6

(Q) What proportion should the cinnamon be?
(A) Regular cinnamon water, as may be obtained . . . that give for an activity or a settling and an easing of the tissues in the stomach itself.   19-4

Cinnamon has been prized throughout antiquity. First imported to Egypt in 2000 BC, the fragrant spice was used in the embalming process and was one of several ingredients of *kyphi*, a form of incense.

Rich in antioxidants, cinnamon may help regulate blood sugar and provide much needed anti–inflammatory agents that can benefit your heart and ward off cancers. Even in the reading above, we see Source recommending it for helping with nerve pain. Cinnamon is good for that, and so much more.

Frankincense

So they represent in the metaphysical sense the three phases of man's experience in materiality; gold, the material; frankincense, the ether or ethereal; myrrh, the healing force as brought with same; or body, mind, soul.   5749-7

The entity brought the frankincense and gave same to the Master at that period.   256-1

Frankincense is mentioned seven times in the life readings relating to the birth of Christ.

The first reading in this section is really amazing in that Cayce is speaking to someone about the symbolism of the Three Wise Men from the Bible and likening them to the ideas we've discussed earlier of material, mind, and spirit.

Juniper

Now we find there are many abnormal conditions in this body. These conditions that may be corrected for there are some that have become abnormal for this body, have to do with eliminations . . . Add two oz. alcohol, with thirty minims oil of juniper . . .
                    126-1

According to Web MD, juniper oil is used for digestion problems to treat everything from bloating and gas to urinary tract infections, so it is truly amazing Cayce tuned into that fact by citing juniper as a key for helping with eliminations.

Myrrh

Well were those conditions attended to in that of the physical, by massaging well into the sacral and the lower portion of the cerebrospinal system, equal parts of olive oil and tincture of myrrh. Heat the oil, adding the myrrh to same, using only sufficient to massage for each treatment. This may be done once or twice each day. This will be found strengthening and beneficial toward the entity gaining its physical strength, and in the correction of those conditions necessary to bring about the healing properties in these portions of body by that increased circulation to these parts.   136-60

Myrrh was mentioned over a thousand times in the life readings. In particular, Cayce recommended numerous times that olive oil and tincture of myrrh to be massaged into the body to assist eliminations. Important in antiquity, myrrh was used by the Egyptians to embalm mummies and as incense, which we will look at next.

Incense

THESE then, made for that as ye have in thine experiences in the present expressed: First in cleanliness, in purifying of the body, in the washing in blood, in water, that ye may be purified before thyself first and then before others. The anointing with the incense . . .   281-25

Using smoke to clear energy is an ancient technique used by indigenous tribes and ancient peoples for thousands of years. Passing through fragrant smoke to wash off the influences and vibrations of the outer world actually removes stuck energy and clears the material, mental, and spiritual fields around the body so that you are clear when you enter sacred space. I've used incense for years to create sacred space in my healing room and at home. Egyptians used the pleasing scent of incense to honor the gods as part of the rituals in the temples.

Part 2: Mental/Mind

Cleansing the Faults

. . . making for the raising of that ye know as thine senses or perception or consciousness of the activities to all the faults, by comparison, as arose among others.   281-25

As to the manner of the service there: The individuals having cleansed themselves of those appendages that hindered, came not merely for the symbolic understanding. For these, to be sure, were all symbolized—the faults . . .   281-25

Once we've opened up our channels to the life source called breath, it's time to release some of the deeper aspects that may be hindering our progress in life. In the Temple of Sacrifice as Cayce describes, these faults may have been more physical in nature:

. . . This priest, this Ra-Ta, attempted to eradicate same; in that manner as might be compared to the hospitalization in the present, where individuals—through the lack of the proper application of the physical laws—have allowed growths, tumors, cancers, those things or conditions in the body—stones in various portions of the organism; and the necessity—as considered in the present—of operative measures to remove growths of various characters throughout the system . . .   2072-8

While our current faults might not need a physical removal, there is such a thing as thoughtforms, which are physical yet invisible energy blockages that affect all of us. They get stuck in our energetic fields, our etheric bodies we discussed earlier in the book. These thoughtforms can wreak havoc on us at an unseen level and must be cleared for us to achieve our highest potential.

Working as an energy healer for years, I've been exposed to the idea of thoughtforms and after studying the readings, I believe Cayce may have been one of the first to mention this concept in the readings about Atlantis. According to Cayce, as humanity evolved, there was a time in history when people communicated through thought alone before evolving into material reality. In one reading, he tells a woman that she lived at a critical time in the Atlantean era when this transition was taking place:

> . . . the entity was in the Atlantean period, during those greater upheavals in the land, from the first and the beginning of the second destruction of the greater body of the continent. The entity then was among those who were the rulers, or the higher class of people in that particular sphere; giving much in the interpretation of those activities throughout the period; understanding much as to the CHANGES that were wrought through the changing from the thought form to the various associations with the MATERIAL things during that period . . .   268-3

It's unfortunate that many people are not more aware of the physical space that thoughts take in our energy fields. This is something that is not widely known or taught in the mainstream, yet it is something I believe is real.

Some thoughtforms could be incredibly positive. You may receive a compliment about how good you are at something, take it to heart, and allow that to lead you in a certain direction, fueled and motivated by that positivity.

On the other hand, some thoughtforms are anything but positive. You were insulted or teased, and you say you brushed it off, but have you? I believe every person alive has a story to tell about someone who hurt them deeply with words, and while we may believe we let it go and moved on, I know for a fact after working with people over the years that it is these very hurts that cause lasting damage to our soul journeys and life paths. If we could remove the thoughtforms completely and replace those energies with love and light, we would be better for it.

Each of us is connected to the other; we are all part of the whole—the divine all that is, and yet, we all express ourselves in totally unique ways that are one-of-a-kind. For this reason, I cannot tell you what your faults are that you must clear in this section.

That said, I believe I can help you identify the proper things to work on—at least for now. I hope you'll find these processes of such value that from time to time you'll want to come back and do them again. Our energy bodies are like onions, and when we peel back a few layers, there're always more underneath! What this means is that as long as we're here on earth in a physical body, we have work to do. Not to worry! All we can do is the best we can at any given moment. The unfolding is like the bloom of a flower. Each day is new and exciting as you open up to higher forms of peace and happiness.

Finding Fault

In this next section we will clear out what Cayce calls the symbols of faults. The idea of reading a book to find out your faults seems a little, well, unmotivating, right? These days, our perfection–obsessed society wants us to look and feel perfectly gorgeous one hundred percent of the time. Not only is that not possible, it isn't healthy either! Please give yourself a break, literally, and extend kindness to the person looking back at you in the mirror each day. Wouldn't you agree you're doing the best you can? Lighten up on yourself! You're a wonderful person!

Just as we can gradually learn to love and be kinder to ourselves, I know that deep down within every one of us, myself included, there is some negative self–talk. We aren't smart enough, handsome enough, brave enough, whatever. A lot of times these *limiting beliefs*, as we'll call them, are things you heard growing up from either a well–meaning (but wrong!) parent or from some bully on the playground. Over time, they evolve into vicious space-wasting thoughtforms that need to be cleared.

Letting it Out

I know this is going to be a little tough, but I want you to get a piece of paper and jot down some of the things you heard or saw in the past that you're still bothered by today. You may not know what those are right now because over time, they've been pushed down and stuffed away so you can function in daily life, and that's okay. For some people, it might take a few days before you start to remember the things that hurt. On the other hand, you might not only remember, but know exactly when that happened and be able to recite the words verbatim.

Remember that when I am talking about *faults*, much of the time these may not even be real. They're simply hurtful statements pointed out to you by people along the way. They might actually have been jealous of you, or perhaps they had pain in their own life and decided to take it out on someone, and you just happened to be the recipient of their wrath.

I'll share one of mine with you. When I was a kid, they called me "the mouth," because if you've ever seen me, I do have a huge mouth. Ouch! That hurt just writing that! You learn to laugh it off, but it still stings, even after all these years. The fact of the matter is that it's true, but the way people said it wasn't the nicest.

Painful things like this happen to everybody. Just the other day, I was out at an event and someone in our group started talking about mean things kids used to say to him. They called him a terrible name I cannot repeat here, and he said it was because he had lost all his teeth in his mouth due to an illness. He eventually had most of them reconstructed, but the force in which he spoke told me that it was still painful, even after so many years.

His poignant confession led to just about everyone in the group going around and sharing all the horrible things they'd heard about themselves through the years. One woman said someone told her she had an awful speaking voice, so she went out and started a radio show. Another person was told he was a nerd and was ostracized in school, but now works as a successful scientist. And as for me, *the mouth*, I've been able to use my mouth quite successfully over the years despite its size.

The conversation lasted quite a while, and I think everyone got a lot out of hearing other people's stories because it reminded us all that every single person has problems; everyone encounters difficulties; and despite that, there was a feeling of wanting to prove others wrong, rise above, and succeed despite obstacles. I think that's powerful for people to hear every so often. Sharing difficulties and how you overcame them can be incredibly affirming. One thing I've learned over the years is that when you're down, there's only one way to go, and that's up. Have faith and things will come around sooner or later. They have to!

Comedians are a great example of what I'm talking about. Think of your favorite comedian. Many of the most successful comics have a repertoire of jokes where they basically make fun of themselves. Under–

neath the comedy, you can usually find a fragile person taking personal hurts to a public forum to work them out. It may not be always the case, but think about this the next time you see a comedian.

Now you. Go ahead. Nobody's looking. Just jot something down. Pull it up out of your subconscious and get it on the paper. That simple act alone will be an amazing healer! Take however long you need to make a list, check it twice and then we can do a clearing that I believe you will find quite liberating.

Next, we'll do a little exercise to clear this out and raise the frequency by releasing the charge you have on that old energy. When you do this or any of the exercises in this book, you can record this journey and play it back to yourself. There are several excellent apps you can download for free that work great for this purpose. That way you can listen as often as you'd like. Another benefit is the fact your subconscious mind loves to hear the sound of your voice. Consciously, I'm not always a fan of listening to myself, and I know many people feel the same way, but at the deeper levels, when you speak to yourself, it has an incredibly powerful impact.

Let's get started!

Exercise

Go ahead and sit in a comfortable chair, feet on the floor, hands in your lap. Close your eyes. Feel a beautiful healing beam of pure white light coming down in through the top of your head. Allow the light to move down, down, down your spine, through your arms and legs, and into your feet.

Feel the light getting stronger as it pours out your heart, creating a golden ball of light that surrounds you by three feet in all directions.

Imagine you're there, floating in the light and you see or feel the person or people who said hurtful things to you in the past, people who pointed out faults. See them there.

Now allow them to tell you once again what they said back then. Imagine they point out a fault. Once they do, imagine they are holding your fault in their hands and you can see it. Have them hand it to you now.

What does it look like? What color is it? See it, feel it, know it is there in physical form. Hold it and notice that as you do, the fault gets smaller and smaller until it is the size of a piece of dust. Blow the speck of dust into the air and watch while it disappears. It's gone, forever! Good job!

Now allow the person or people to apologize for hurting your feelings. Notice that they tell you they are sorry and that they were only doing the best they could at that time. Take your time and let them say what they need to say.

Imagine as you've released your fault and it has disappeared that you hear their words of apology and that you feel lighter than before—more at peace, happier, healthier. Very good.

Next, imagine that you can forgive them. You can easily forgive their trespasses. Feel yourself release this energy by opening to the healing power of forgiveness.

Allow your subconscious mind and Higher Self to remind you of all the ways you benefited from the lessons learned from this experience. Did you overcome adversity? Did you find compassion for others who were in your same predicament? Allow memories, thoughts, and feelings to come into your mind. Notice what you notice. Although this was not a pleasant experience at the time, can you see how it made you grow as a person? Good job!

Thank the people who hurt your feelings for all the lessons you learned from the experience. Imagine feeling gratitude for the insights and soul growth and notice how much lighter and better you feel. Allow this light to extend to them and watch as they float up, up, and away. Good job. Now open your eyes, feeling awake and better than you did before.

How was that? I hope you feel lighter and better as a result of that clearing. Remember, it might take a couple of times, but know that you are awesome and making great progress!

Uncovering Emotions

Next, we'll look into the realm of the mind. Earlier we talked about the three layers to your field and in the second layer is your emotional energy stored.

In order to shift this area, you need to ask yourself what emotions cripple you?

Let me point out that procrastination is NOT an emotion! If you are a procrastinator, as I can be at times, ask yourself what causes you to put things off?

A lot of times it's fear, even though it may not appear to be fear when you're right in the middle of a situation. Maybe you're afraid of working too hard, getting exhausted, criticized by your peers, who knows! It could be any number of things.

Perhaps you're angry at a family member, coworker, or the society in general.

You might even be jealous of so-in-so who got that big promotion at work. Who knows! You might feel any or all of these and then some, and all at the same time.

Are you lonely? Sad? Depressed? I think this is all too common these days thanks to technology. What else do you feel when nobody's looking? What feelings are hard to admit, even to yourself? Go ahead and write down anything and everything that comes to mind.

Uncovering Your Emotions to Take Stock of Them

It's not easy to sit quietly with yourself long enough to hear the quiet voice that's speaking to you, but it can be incredibly transformational when you do. Take time to find out what's stored deep down inside of yourself so you can do something about it. Whatever you feel, remember that your emotions can't bite unless you stuff them down into a deep, dark place where you can't find them.

The societal expectation of needing to be perfect all the time is one of the biggest challenges we're faced with today. It's not possible to be flawless when we're living in a human body working through our life lessons. So, go easy on yourself but make a list of anything you're feeling. Take your time; there's no right or wrong. Just see what comes up.

Keep your list handy for future reference, and then narrow it down to the top three emotions you're feeling right now. List them in order of severity, for example: Anger, Sadness, Fear . . . or whatever order you feel best represents your true state of mind. You can always come back to any other emotions later, but in this next exercise, we're going to do a short clearing on the top three emotions you uncovered.

Clearing Exercise

Find a comfortable place to sit, close your eyes, and go into a meditative position with feet flat on the floor and your hands in your lap.

Take a deep breath in through your nose and exhale out your mouth. With every breath, begin to relax more and more.

Now imagine that you can recall the first emotion you uncovered and put it out in your hands. *What color is it? How does it feel? Talk to the emotion and ask it what purpose it has for you. Allow it to answer.*

Thank the emotion for playing a part in your journey, but tell it that you must now be released so you can climb to new levels.

In a moment when I count to three, you will release the emotion. Three, two, one, release! Imagine the emotion is floating away, into the air.

Notice that there is a beam of light connecting you with this emotion as it flies away. On the count of three, that cord will be cut. One, two, three, cut the cord and allow the emotion to disappear into a cloud of light. Very good.

Now go on to the next emotion. Ready? Notice that emotion and put it out in your hands. What color is it? How does it feel? Talk to the emotion and ask it what purpose it has for you. Allow it to answer.

Thank the emotion for playing a part in your journey, but tell it that you must now be released so you can climb to new levels.

In a moment when I count to three, you will release the emotion. Three, two, one, release! Imagine the emotion is floating away, into the air.

Notice that there is a beam of light connecting you with this emotion as it flies away. On the count of three, that cord will be cut. One, two, three, cut the cord and allow the emotion to disappear into a cloud of light. Very good.

Finally, go on to the third emotion. Notice that emotion and put it out on your hands. What color is it? How does it feel? Talk to the emotion and ask it what purpose it has for you. Allow it to answer.

Thank the emotion for playing a part in your journey, but tell it that you must now be released so you can climb to new levels.

In a moment when I count to three, you will release the emotion. Three, two, one, release! Imagine the emotion is floating away, into the air.

Notice there is a beam of light connecting you with this emotion as it flies away. On the count of three, that cord will be cut. One, two, three, cut the cord and allow the emotion to disappear into a cloud of light. Very good.

Now imagine that you can notice how much lighter you feel and, in a moment, when I count to three, you will come back into the room. Ready? Three, two, one, and you're back!

How did that go? Do you feel lighter?

If necessary, keep working with this exercise, releasing all you need to release.

Self-Talk

Now that we've addressed ridding yourself of the unwanted thought-forms from things other people have said to you and the appendage of negative emotion, we need to discuss next what you're *saying to yourself*. That's even harder to identify sometimes, but so powerful!

Hopefully you're telling yourself what an awesome, unique, powerful, creative person you are, but if you're not, then it's good to get rid of self-talk that's not serving you anymore. What are you telling yourself, under your breath? Whose voice is in your head?

Many of my clients report that they have a parent from childhood who told them they were no good, a slob, or a kid at school said they were a slow runner, or clumsy. You name it; it's probably been said to someone over the course of history. Unfortunately, this data sticks in our minds and over the years can become heavier on our spirit than carrying a backpack filled with steel. These are more examples of the thoughtforms that other people have sent to us, but over time, that voice of our teacher or bully can morph into our own voice as we begin believing what others told us.

Write down anything you say to yourself such as, "I'm no good at this or that," or "I can't because of this or that..." and fill in the blank.

Again, I hope your list isn't too long, but at most, narrow it down to the top three things you're saying to yourself, or hearing, that are not serving you anymore.

This is not necessarily something you can do off the top of your head. Begin with jotting down whatever comes into your mind, but you might want to sit with this for a day or two and then see what you come up with.

Pay attention when things aren't going perfectly and how you react. Are you down on yourself? Are you overwhelmed or sleepy? Then what do you tell yourself about that?

Once you have your list of your top three detrimental examples of self-talk, you're ready to let them go.

Next, we're going to do a quick exercise to release things that are no longer serving you.

Exercise

Go ahead and sit in a comfortable chair with your feet flat on the floor, your hands in your lap.

Close your eyes and take a deep breath in through your nose, exhale out your mouth. Take another deep breath and with each breath you take, you feel more and more relaxed. Very good.

Now imagine you can notice the first example of self-talk that is no longer serving you. Go ahead and see it spelled out, hear it, or just sense it. How does that make you feel?

Imagine as you notice it, you can see it in physical form in front of you. Notice there is an energetic cord connecting you with those words, and when I count to three, you will cut the cord and release yourself from these words. Ready? Three, two, one, cut the cord.

Feel a healing white light surrounding you, raising your frequency, and bringing you love and peace. Good job.

Now go to the next example of self-talk that is no longer serving you. Go ahead and see it spelled out, hear it, or just sense it. How does that make you feel?

Imagine as you notice it, you can see it in physical form in front of you. Notice there is an energetic cord connecting you with those words, and when I count to three, you will cut the cord and release yourself from these words. Ready? Three, two, one, cut the cord.

Feel a healing white light surrounding you, raising your frequency, and bringing you love and peace. Good job.

Finally, go to the third example of self-talk that is no longer serving you. Go ahead and see it spelled out, hear it, or just sense it. How does that make you feel?

Imagine as you notice it, you can see it in physical form in front of you. Notice that there is an energetic cord connecting you with those words, and when I count to three, you will cut the cord and release yourself from these words. Ready? Three, two, one, cut the cord.

Feel a healing white light surrounding you, raising your frequency, and bringing you love and peace. Good job.

Notice with each phrase you release, you feel lighter and brighter than ever before. Imagine that this white light is filled with love, joy, and peace and that your energy is getting brighter and brighter, lighter and lighter. Good job!

In a moment when I count to three, you will return to your space feeling lighter and better than before. One, two, and three, you're back!

How did that feel? You might want to repeat this process for any other things you notice coming up, and over time, I'm sure you'll find this is incredibly helpful. That's my hope for you!

Part 3: Spiritual

Symbols of Virtue

. . . For these, to be sure, were all symbolized—the faults, the virtues of man . . .   281-25

We cannot bring up the negative and clear that out without replacing those things with better, higher frequency information. We all have virtues, and in this section, you are going to identify your strengths and use them to greater advantage.

The Cayce readings talk about the symbols of virtue being part of the healing rituals found in the Temple Beautiful.

In the last sections, you've released your faults and negative self-talk, so it makes sense that we would want to replace those with things you do want.

Just as before, I'd like you to sit down with pen and paper or your phone or computer and jot down your very best qualities. I know it's not always polite to brag about ourselves, but you have great qualities that I know others have pointed out to you, so it's time to start taking stock. Even Cayce mentioned the fact that you should be free of ego, yet promote yourself as long as it is in alignment with God:

> (Q) Who is the best person or what is the best channel for me to work through for my development and promotion? (A) SELF— and God; and taking Him into partnership with you, in the directions with you—that's the only way for advancement! For all power and all might, that may be in the hands of man, is only lent for a purpose; for it IS of God.   1388-1

Are you loyal, sincere, empathetic, kind, generous, virtuous, giving, selfless? The list goes on and on, right? Please take a little time and think about what you believe are your very best gifts that you're giving to the world at this time. And please, don't be shy!

It's hard for us to sing our own praises at times, so if you can't think of anything yourself, then think back on what others have told you. Were you a lifesaver? Did you selflessly give of your time or other resources? Are you courageous or creative? Our friends and associates are mirrors of our own journey, and we often need others not only to put us in our place but also to remind us that we have wonderful qualities which are sorely needed on our planet at this time.

As with the last exercise, write down all of your good qualities and then narrow them down to the top three virtues. Once that's done, we will do a connecting exercise to tune into the high frequency of our own awesomeness.

Exercise

Sit in your comfortable chair and close your eyes. Rest your hands in your lap and your feet on the floor. Breathe. Feel a loving white light traveling down through the top of your head, through your spine, your arms and legs, and into your feet.

Imagine that this light is surrounding you in a beautiful ball of white that heals and protects you while raising up your energies to the highest level.

Now imagine that you can recall one of your virtues. Imagine that this virtue is floating up to you now. What color is it? How big is it? Go ahead now and allow that virtue to float up to you and float right inside your heart. Feel that energy expanding in your heart, moving into every cell in your being—your heart, your lungs, your neck and shoulders, your legs and feet, arms and hands, your head, and into your mind. Allow that virtue to expand until it pours out of your cells and joins with that white ball of light, becoming brighter and lighter than before. Good job.

Now imagine that you can recall another one of your virtues. Imagine that this virtue is floating up to you now. What color is it? How big is it? Go ahead now and allow that virtue to float up to you and float right inside your heart. Feel that energy expanding in your heart, moving into every cell in your being—your heart, your lungs, your neck and shoulders, your legs and feet, arms and hands, your head, and into your mind. Allow that virtue to expand until it pours out of your cells and joins with that white ball of light, becoming brighter and lighter than before. Notice that you are twice as light and twice as bright as you were before. Feeling light and free, joyful and peaceful. Good job.

Now imagine that you can recall your third major virtue. Imagine that this virtue is floating up to you now. What color is it? How big is it? Go ahead now and allow that virtue to float up to you and float right inside your heart. Feel that energy expanding in your heart, moving into every cell in your being—your heart, your lungs, your neck and shoulders, your legs and feet, arms and hands, your head, and into your mind. Allow that virtue to expand until it pours out of your cells and joins with that white ball of light, becoming brighter and lighter than before. Allow this virtue to intermingle with the other two to make you lighter and brighter, happier and more peaceful than you've ever been before. Good job.

Now take all of this new light and notice that your energy frequencies are lighter than they've ever been before; in a moment, when I count to three, you will come back knowing that you will take this new energy with you now and always, and understand that you are feeling better than ever before. Three, two, one, you're back!

How do you feel? Ready to go out and take on the world? I hope! Remember you have much to give to the world, so own it and move forward with joy!

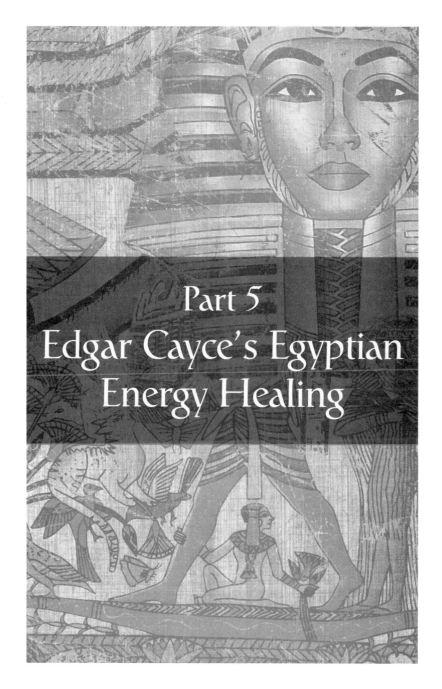

Part 5
Edgar Cayce's Egyptian Energy Healing

All of the exploration we've done so far all comes down to this—learning how to do the Edgar Cayce's Egyptian Energy Healing process. First, we will explore some healing symbols; then you'll learn several ways to do this yourself.

Healing Symbols and Meanings

Cayce mentioned several symbols that will be used in ECEEH. Earlier in the book we discussed channeling symbols for healing. Symbols are used as shortcuts for your subconscious mind and can help you focus your intention for the energy you send to another person. In the Edgar Cayce's Egyptian Energy Healing system, Cayce and Source left us passages about symbols used in the times of Ra–Ta that we are going to use to raise the vibrations in and around the physical body.

In the past several years since I first began working as a healer, our planetary energy has shifted dramatically. Techniques that worked wonders earlier in my career don't seem to do much anymore. Totally new energy is needed to make shifts. Some of the techniques I was shown when working with ECEEH are quite different from anything I've used in the past and hope they will be helpful to you.

When this set of symbols is delivered using the technique I will show you, they bring tremendous balance to the recipient, even during these unstable times.

The visual images you see of each of these symbols were shown to me in my inner mind, and I drew them as how I saw them. One way to work with the system is to learn to draw the symbols exactly how you see them pictured here, but you can also visualize the whole symbol in its entirety in your mind's eye and it's just as effective. Intent is the key. Let's take a look at the symbols now.

Lamp of the Light Bearers = Illumination

. . . For these, to be sure, were all symbolized . . . in the light or
the lamp borne by those who served as the Light Bearers to those
who entered for their initiation, or for their preparation to be that
as given by the teachers—even RA-TA.   281-25

Light Bearers served as Temple initiates and shared their knowledge
and healing with others to assist them on the path of enlightenment.
Cayce is clear that this important group shared a symbol and in ECEEH,
this symbol will open the healing session.

For those who have Reiki training, in that system and many others,
you somehow have to set your intention to begin the healing session
and let your spirit guides and the universe know you are about to
conduct a healing. Because this group of Light Bearers initiated these
healings, what better way to open your session than by visualizing the
symbol of the Lamp?

If you're brand new to energy healing, another way to see the Lamp
is to think of a book. All books, even this one, have an introduction
where the author sets the stage for what you are about to read. Think
of the Lamp as the introductory chapter to open the door to your mind
so you can get going with the contents in a more informed way.

In healing, we always have to set the intention of what we are about to do, and the Lamp calls in all the unseen help you need to get the ECEEH started. Cayce seems to place great importance on the Lamp symbol as an essential part of Temple rituals, and as I have been working with the ECEEH system, it is a critical step for the process to achieve the best results.

Lamps and lights have obvious symbolic qualities of raising vibrations, eliminating darkness, and allowing high-frequency light to flow through the energy fields of those receiving healing. Opening any healing session with an influx of light makes sense, and this modality is no exception. I think of the Lamp symbol as a call to reawaken all the helpful forces from the Light Bearers of the past and to enlist their assistance through the journey of self-healing. All time is now, so we can call on these initiates and know they are assisting us in our journey.

Additionally, when you think about it, we are all Light Bearers. Everyone who is called to do healing work for others is a modern beacon of hope, peace, and light. So, when you call on the Lamp, think of it as your cosmic calling card that assists you in activating and opening your energy. You are, in effect, saying to the Universal Manager, "Yes, I am ready and allow light to pass through me so I can be a channel and help to other beings." Once you call out and enlist divine help, the Lamp symbol is used to open all energy fields, chakras, and etheric bodies and to burn off or eliminate any lower frequencies or unwanted energies.

Each symbol we will work with has a keynote or a one-word description to guide you in your intentions while working with the energy. Some of these keynotes were given to us directly from Source, while others were given to me while working with the system. The Lamp keynote is illumination because you have to see where you are going by illuminating your path in order to move forward. Lamp sets the stage and opens the door for the next steps. You will be doing this yourself very soon, but for now, let's take a look at the other symbols and their meanings.

Seven Stages of Man's Development Symbols

(Q) What were the symbols of the seven stages of man's development?

(A) The world as the beetle. Birth as the cockerel. The Mind as
the serpent. Wisdom as the hawk. The varied activities in the
cross, the crown, the gate, the door, the way.   281-25

The remainder of the ECEEH system will work with several other
symbols specifically mentioned in the Cayce readings that also had
ties to the times in ancient Egypt. Source listed symbols representing
each of the Seven Stages of Man's Development, and these symbols
transform the frequencies of initiates and take people to higher levels
of consciousness.

When I saw these symbols, I immediately recognized that they
would be useful tools for modern seekers, and apparently, I was not
the first person to think so. In one life reading, someone wanted further
clarification about the seven stages symbols, but Source refused, citing
the fact that the healing work itself was more important:

(Q) In the seven stages of man's development, why is the beetle
the symbol of the world, the cockerel as birth, the serpent as the
mind, the hawk as wisdom? [281-25, Par. 34-A]
(A) We are going far afield. Keep rather to the spiritual healing.
                                                                  281-26

I understand and appreciate the spirit of what Source said here. We
should not get too caught up in symbols or too attached to objects.
Instead, we should have faith that this information was presented for a
reason, and we should just do the work, knowing that if we call in the
energies and do the spiritual healing, then the right information will
go to the recipient. All will be well.

Still, for our current purposes of ECEEH, we must know what these
symbols mean so we can correctly focus our intentions. The moment
I saw the reading, I experienced a download of sorts and knew what
they meant and how to work with them. After following these inner
directions and working with the symbols for quite a while now, both
on myself and others, I've found them to be quite amazing for raising
frequencies. The reading lists the symbols in order for a reason, and
when you think of how Cayce interprets the keynotes for each one, the
symbols are presented in the order of the soul's journey through time.

Beetle = World

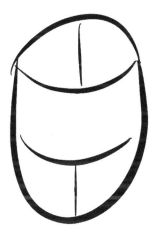

The world as the beetle. 281-25

Yet these may ye eat of every flying creeping thing that goeth upon all four, which have legs above their feet, to leap withal upon the earth; even these of them ye may eat; the locust after his kind, and the bald locust after his kind, and the beetle after his kind . . . Leviticus: 11:21-23

Beetle is the world, our connection to the planet and to each other. Using the Beetle as a symbol for the world makes sense since the Egyptians saw the scarab beetle as a symbol for Khepri, the solar deity representing the early morning dawn. Scarabs rolled their dung into balls from east to west, and ancient people viewed that as a symbol of the sun rolling across the sky, representing new life or a new dawn. Scarab carvings have since appeared in numerous funerary accoutrements, often placed over the heart of the deceased, and to the Egyptians, scarabs represented the turning of the world, rebirth, purification, evolvement, and resurrection—all of which can be considered when using this transformative symbol. Once the light of the Lamp opens the energy fields, Beetle works to establish our connection to each other on a cellular level, thus opening us up for further transformation.

Cockerel = Birth

Birth as the cockerel.   281-25

Upon the right side put the small symbol as of a rooster; this as the figure of a game cock or the like; this in color, not in white, but in color; not as crowing, but head erect . . .   533-20

Jesus said unto him, Verily I say unto thee, That this night, before the cock crow, thou shalt deny me thrice. Matthew 26:33-34

The Cockerel is a term that refers to a mature male rooster that is less than one year old. Many Christians believe the rooster is the symbol for Christ as it is reported to be the first animal to announce the birth of Jesus. The rooster also crowed when Peter denied Jesus three times.

The symbolism of the rooster is important and far reaching in ancient cultures around the world. In China, the rooster appears in the zodiac as a person with great enthusiasm for life. In alchemy, the rooster signifies that the conjunction, or sacred marriage or joining of two forces, has begun. Seen as the bringer of dawn and light, the Cockerel seems an obvious choice for Source to view as representative of birth.

In healing terms, Cockerel as birth represents the new influx of energy flowing in as we come into the world. Light clearing a path for the new being who incarnated, the Beetle establishes our connection to everyone else, and Cockerel announces our arrival and further preparation on our healing journey. I've found the Cockerel symbol also quite helpful with opening the throat chakra center because of the ability of Cockerels to speak clearly.

Serpent = Mind

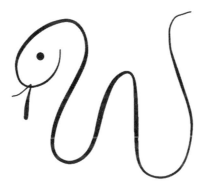

The Mind as the serpent.   281-25

And Moses and Aaron went in unto Pharaoh, and they did so as the Lord had commanded: and Aaron cast down his rod before Pharaoh, and before his servants, and it became a serpent. Exodus 7:10

The serpent has played an important symbolic role in cultures throughout the ages, particularly in Biblical times as well as in ancient Egypt. The Egyptian goddess Wadjet was depicted as a cobra and had an all-seeing eye which represented wisdom and all knowingness, an appropriate choice for the mind symbol as it relates to the Egyptian times. She was often depicted coiled atop the head of sun god Ra as a

protector. You may be most familiar with Wadjet from the golden funerary mask of King Tutankhamen. She is depicted there at his forehead
with Nekhbet the vulture.

To say that the serpent represents Mind implies that the mind is not
stagnant but expanding and becoming illuminated. On the path of human development, after birth, the individual begins to develop mental
aptitude; Source says that is represented by the serpent. If you're familiar with the concept of Kundalini energy, the Serpent symbol can also
represent the dormant life-force energy coiled at the base of the spine,
ready to be awakened. When using this symbol, the Serpent travels up
and down the body, opening up the access to our incredible life-force.

Hawk = Wisdom

Wisdom as the hawk.   281-25

. . . the hawk, or the figure with the hawk face or head (and this
in flesh, though head in brown and gray)—do not make the bill
too long.   379-18

Doth the hawk fly by thy wisdom, and stretch her wings toward
the south? Job 39:26

Once the mind is developed, over time wisdom is the result; hence the Hawk symbol, according to Source, represents the fine tuning of mind into a higher state of being. Source could have cited the hawk's relation to wisdom through the above-mentioned Bible verse, or through the fact that Horus, son of Osiris and Isis, and the Eye of Horus symbolize protection.

Although Horus is technically a falcon, because of the falcon's close relationship to the hawk, the two may be synonymous in terms of Cayce's information. Another reason why I believe this symbol refers to Horus is because the hawk image I visualized was startlingly similar to the Egyptian hieroglyph for Horus. That's proof enough for me, even though hawks and falcons are not the same breed of bird, hawks lived in the region at that time.

For healing purposes, this symbol works with the heart energy, enlivening our passion for living and raises loving energies in the light bodies.

Cross = Life

The varied activities in the cross . . .   281-25

First, the entity should have more of the colors of BLUE about the body; and those characters that represent the Egyptian cross—which, as seen, is more or less in that form of the lazy or the Maltese, except open and crosswise.   620-1

Then said Jesus unto his disciples, If any man will come after me, let him deny himself, and take up his cross, and follow me. Matthew 16:24

Cayce was quite specific for the earlier symbols and what they represented. Knowing what a symbol's keynote is can be quite useful in healing. In Reiki for example, Cho Ku Rei is a power symbol. Likewise, after working with each of these symbols, I was guided to provide you with a one-word description for the final symbols in our set. We can certainly ponder why Cayce chose to not specifically mention the descriptions of these himself; perhaps it is because he assumes that we already understand what Crosses and Crowns are all about.

Know then that the keynotes for the next few symbols represent what I was guided to provide you, but all healers who work on their craft over time know that symbols and meanings can shift and change depending on the recipient of the energy. The most important aspect is intent, and the keynotes are meant as guideposts to begin your journey in working with the energy.

Source called this symbol a Cross, and since this is based on Egypt, I was intuitively guided to use the ankh, even though Cayce never mentioned ankh in the life readings, other than as a part of the name of Pharaoh Tutankhamen. In ancient Egypt, the ankh was the symbol for life. Only Pharaohs carried the symbol, which represented the fact that they had the power to both give life and take it away.

Source is quite vague about the meaning of the Cross, other than to say this symbol means: "The varied activities in the cross . . . " (281-25) What activity might Source mean? To me, the cross represents our religious or spiritual life, which is a part of most people's activities, which is why Life is the keynote for this symbol.

When working with ECEEH, you will find, as I did, that certain symbols resonate more with you than others. The Cross symbol can be quite powerful for some healers, particularly those who lived in Egypt in past lives.

Crown = Power

The varied activities in . . . the crown . . .   281-25

And they made the plate of the holy crown of pure gold, and wrote upon it a writing, like to the engravings of a signet, HOLINESS TO THE LORD. Exodus 39:30

The crown symbol is taken (per my intuition) from part of a drawing of what a cross would look like in Egyptian hieroglyphs. I was guided to make these drawings as simplified as possible.

The Crown is undoubtedly a symbol of power, hence the keynote. There are different ways to view power. Source might be referring to the secular power we all must face in the world, whether we are striving to achieve it for ourselves or struggling to rise above it. This personal power, so to speak, is an aspect of everyone's life, regardless of where you're from. In the above reading, where Source says the Crown related to varied activities, I believe this represents the more secular or ego-driven aspects of the person and our ability to maintain self-esteem while bringing our ego energies under control.

When I was shown what symbol to use for this system, I felt guided to use part of one of the Egyptian hieroglyphs that represents the crowns worn by various Pharaohs. The swirl used here happens to be part of the Deshret, the Red Crown, symbolizing Lower (northern) Egypt. Interestingly, Ra-Ta and his followers settled in the lower part of Egypt, long before unification of the two sections. Another hieroglyph called

Hedjet, or the White Crown, represents Lower Egypt and another called Pschent is a hieroglyph that represents the unified land with both the White and Red crowns combined.

For our healing purposes, I've found this Crown symbol quite powerful for balancing the areas around the solar plexus and sacral chakra centers which are the seat of our personal and sexual power and our ability to put ourselves forth in the world. You will have a chance to work with these symbols soon enough, and you will likely gain your own insights into how all of these symbols feel and are used.

Gate/Door = Ascension

The varied activities in the gate, the door . . .   281-25

A gate or door represents the threshold into another space or area, and as such, this symbol opens the door to leaving the mundane world behind and accessing higher realms and frequencies. During my research, I found the hieroglyph for the Door and when I began working with that image, I found it to be incredibly amazing and had intuitive insights through dreams and visions that this was the correct image to use for this symbol. When Source says, " . . . the gate, the door, the way . . . ," since he spoke of only seven symbols, we can only assume these three words are synonyms meaning the same thing. I was guided to divide them further though and use the term Way to describe the final step in the system.

The idea of a doorway suggests raising vibrational frequencies and consciousness, so the person achieves a higher level of awareness and graduates into the new reality as a result of undergoing the previous steps. In personal–development teachings, the threshold might symbolize death, lifting into the heavens, transitioning into the final stages of life in preparation for ascension. By death, I do not mean physical death, per se, but symbolic death—letting go of outdated influences and rising into a new state of being.

The Ascension keynote implies the simple truth that all healing work is transcendental in its very nature because the fields around the body are not the same once the processes are complete. Each symbol in the ECEEH process builds upon the last, raising the energy higher. My clients all reported varying levels of increased peace and calm after working with the entire system but particularly once they passed through the Gate/Door.

Way = Source

The varied activities in way.   281-25

The final step is called the Way. This process came to me quite clearly after working with ECEEH on myself and on a wonderful group of clients who gave me feedback in the very early stages of the system's development. Remember our Lamp symbol from the first part of ECEEH? The Lamp begins the opening process, and the Way symbol is the original Lamp above the head along with its mirror image appearing under the soles of the feet.

While working with this energy on several people, I kept seeing the Lamp symbol appear over the crown chakra and then a second lamp symbol appeared, spun around, and went down to the soles of the feet right at the end of the session. The image evolved to the symbol pictured above and is still to be seen as the top half over the crown of the head and the bottom half at the soles of the feet. They shift and move together toward the center of the body. You will envision them traveling together and connecting in the midsection near the solar plexus chakra, invigorating the energy field.

In other systems I've taught through the years, there is an idea that we want to work on shifting our energy, so that a state of complete balance and transformation is achieved. By adding the Lamp again over the top of the head in our crown chakra, flipping that same symbol upside down and placing it over the feet is like closing the loop and sealing off this new higher vibration so it stays put and intact, keeping the recipient in a state of grace.

Once the two pieces of the Way symbol merge together in the center of the body, the entire energy field begins to rapidly shift in a counterclockwise direction, and the etheric bodies begin to spin around in a counterclockwise direction. The motion becomes a sort of cosmic turning back of the clock, regenerating the cells, slowing down the aging process and putting more light into the energy fields.

Once the Way symbol begins to spin around, you will wait until it stops which will signify the end of the session. Once this final symbol is introduced, the ascension has occurred and the vibrational energies return to the highest level possible—the love and light we all originated from and forgot once we chose physical incarnation. The return to Source energy concludes the transformation and completes the process. The Way symbol puts the finishing touches on the healing and drastically raises vibrational frequencies in and around the recipient as well as the Light Bearer, or healer.

The first time I experienced this sensation, I realized that although the terms Gate, Door, and Way are synonymous, the final important step of the modality needed to have a name, so although I call it Way, think of this as the Gate/Door opens up the energy bodies to higher frequencies and the Way takes that shift a step further by dramatically raising vibrations even further.

The first time I consciously tried this, I envisioned the first Lamp on the crown of the head and then I saw the inverted Lamp at the feet. Because these symbols are exact opposites, they act like a lid and a container that you and your energy bodies fit into and they fit together perfectly. When you envision this, as I do even when I work on myself, they create an instant ball of white light that surrounds you or the person you're working on, protecting the fields, and setting the perfection in the field so it cannot be disturbed. Since working with this protective bubble of light, I've felt more at ease within myself and have been able to get a lot more done. I feel safe, secure, and protected.

I've talked to a lot of my clients lately who have expressed feelings of fear and needing to be safe. There is a collective energy out in the world now that needs love. We need each other, and we need to feel safe to pursue our purpose. The Way symbol provides a final shield that assists the field in supporting the desire for light and love in our lives. That's it! Now that we've had a brief look at the symbols, let's get into how to work with them.

Ra-Ta Initiation Journey

Under normal circumstances when you take an energy healing course, you would receive an initiation. Later when I show you how to actually do this process, I will have you do a self–healing first so you will basically become energetically attuned into ECEEH without having to come and see me or take a class. That said, I will be teaching this in the future, and I certainly hope to see you there, but in the meantime, this next journey will allow you to travel back to the Temple where you went in Part 4 and meet again with Ra–Ta so he can formally initiate you into the Edgar Cayce's Egyptian Energy Healing modality.

Treat this like a real attunement, so instead of lying down or reclin-

ing, you will sit in a straight–backed chair. Find a time when you won't
be disturbed, and as with all activations in the book, you may want
to find a good recording app for your phone, record this process, then
play it back for yourself. Ready? Let's begin.

Exercise

Sit in a chair with your hands in prayer position and close your eyes.

*Imagine that a beam of pure white light moves through the top of your head,
through your forehead, moving down your spine, into your heart, moving down into
your legs and out the soles of your feet.*

*Allow the light to pour from your heart, creating a beautiful golden ball of light
that surrounds you in all directions. Know that within that golden ball of light, only
that which is of your highest good can come through.*

*Go ahead now and imagine you are standing in front of the Egyptian Temple.
Notice the sign above the doorway which reads:*

LORD, LEAD THOU THE WAY. I COMMIT MY BODY,
MY MIND, TO BE ONE WITH THEE . . .   281-25

*In a moment, when I count to three, you will enter the Temple one, two, and three
. . . walk through the door now. Be there now.*

*Notice that Ra-Ta is there to greet you. He may appear like the modern Edgar
Cayce, or he might have a totally different appearance, but either way, notice him
there and allow him to welcome you inside where you will take a seat.*

*Sitting down now, imagine Ra-Ta is going to initiate you into the healing sym-
bols of this ancient system. During this process, you do not have to see the symbols.
Know that Ra-Ta is activating you into them whether or not you can see them in
your mind's eye.*

*Beginning with the Lamp of the Light Bearers, imagine Ra-Ta places that sym-
bol into your energy field and feel it moving throughout your body from head to
toe. Accept this gift and imagine you can agree to become a Light Bearer now and
always. Very good.*

*Next, the Beetle symbol representing the World moves through every cell in your
being. Then the Cockerel, representing Birth. Feel all of the symbols quickly moving
into your energy fields. Very good. Next, Ra-Ta places Serpent into your field, representing Mind and Hawk representing Wisdom. Allow these symbols to be fully
integrated into your energy field now. Very good.*

Ra-Ta places the Cross, representing Life, into your field, enlivening your own life-force. Next, the Crown amplifies your healing energy and power as it moves through your body in preparation for the Gate/Door symbol. Feel your vibrations increase as you ascend into a higher realm of being. Finally, Ra-Ta carefully places the Way symbol into your field, strengthening you and further raising your vibrations.

Imagine Ra-Ta ends your initiation now. He tells you that you are now fully activated into this healing system. Thank Ra-Ta for providing you with this initiation today, then stand up, make your way back to the Temple door, and walk back out to where you started.

Stand where you first began, noticing you are still surrounded by a golden light. Allow the light to surround your body now and always and notice how much lighter and brighter you feel after your initiation. Know that your energy will increase even more over time and that all is well.

In a moment, when I count to five, you will return into the room having fully received your initiation. Ready? One, coming back into your body, Two, processing this new higher vibrational energy tonight so that by tomorrow morning you are fully integrated into the new system. Three, being safe in all activities, Four, grounded, centered and balanced, and Five, you're back!

I hope you enjoyed your time with Ra-Ta! Next up you will learn how to use the modality after first doing a self-healing that will further integrate you into the new system.

Remember that while it might not feel like you had much of a shift, anytime you work to raise your vibrations and shift energy, it's like receiving a physical massage. Toxins can be released as you let go of the old energy to ascend to the higher level, so drink plenty of water and take great care of yourself using some of the ideas we talked about earlier in the book—gemstones, essential oils, bathing in Epsom salts. You've made a change, and as you begin to do more with this method, you will continue to change your frequency.

You may also want to journal about any thoughts or ideas that happened during your initiation or make note of any special messages received.

How to Do the ECEEH Modality

In this next section I share how to use the symbols. As with all systems, we will cover the four main areas—Self-Healing, Healing Others,

Distance Healing, and Group Healing. I'll also share a couple of other fun techniques you can do using the ECEEH symbols.

Self-Healing

With the return, and with the healing of the body for the greater activities, the entity arose in its thought and power through its application especially in the Temple Beautiful.   1770-2

I'm a big believer in self-healing. How can we assist others if we aren't balanced ourselves? For that reason, it's best to begin by using the ECEEH methods on yourself so you can gain the necessary insights that you will use to help others later on. Even in the times of Ra–Ta, the people who came to the Temple for healing enlisted the help of the Light Bearers who had to practice what they preached by going through extensive preparations and training before they could effectively teach and assist others. We learn by doing.

Normally when you take a class in healing, the instruction is all about working on other people, which is a good thing, because of course, the reason most of us are drawn to the healing arts in the first place is because we have a deep soul calling to serve humanity. I believe that desire is quite noble and worthy. We're taught from an early age to think this way. Still, we must be in a proper place energetically to do so. The perfect analogy is the airplane procedure of putting your oxygen mask on first before helping a child. Likewise, by giving yourself healing first, you are more equipped to serve your fellow beings. Clear yourself first and you become a better version of yourself.

The other reason to do self–healing first is to lead by example. How can you ask other people to do what you haven't done yourself? Makes sense, right? And the byproduct of that action is that you come to the work with a real belief in what you're doing and personal experiences of your triumphs and challenges that can become a true source of inspiration for those whom you're serving. Edgar Cayce's Egyptian Energy Healing is the same. After working with this modality for a while, without a doubt, I believe that by initially working on yourself you will attune to the symbols and frequencies, so it is easier to share. If you've been doing healing work for a while, this modality can be done quite similarly to Reiki or other kinds of healing. Here are some steps I've found helpful to get you started:

1) Setting Sacred Space—Create your sacred space in whatever way makes you feel peaceful and harmonious. You might enjoy soft lighting, gentle music, essential oils, or placing crystals around you. Just make sure the space is inviting and makes you feel comfortable as well as ready to relax and receive. I am a big meditator, so I usually sit in my favorite chair. Sometimes I have my music playing; other times I do not, depending on my mood. Go with the flow and do what feels best. By *sacred space* I mean any energetically purified area where you feel free of distractions and can bring in high vibrations. Some people have altars, while others might sit in their living rooms. Where you do the work isn't as important as *how you feel* while you're there and the intention you set for communing with the divine.

2) Prepare Yourself—Wash your hands and wear clean, comfortable clothes. Again, make sure you feel at ease. Find the most comfortable spot within your designated sacred space to begin. Normally I recommend sitting in a comfortable chair with your feet flat on the floor, but if you have a recliner that you like, that's fine. You can recline with your legs up or lie down on a bed or on the floor, just so long as you feel comfortable and relaxed. If you choose to lie down, do so only if you know you won't fall asleep. Typically, with my hypnosis clients, I insist that they sit because of drowsiness. Do what feels best. If you need to meditate first to get yourself into the right frame of mind, do that, too, if you would like, just so long as you are comfortable and are in the proper space to receive and be a channel for energy.

3) Call in Your Guides—Everybody's different, but I enjoy calling in my guides. I often like to imagine that they are all sitting around me in a semicircle, smiling and sending me loving energy and encouragement. I typically say something aloud like:

"I would like to ask all my guides, angels, and ascended masters who wish to participate today to join me for this healing session."

Then I wait to see who shows up. I could certainly ask Jesus, Mary, and Archangel Michael to come, and I would know they would be there, but they usually do not need to be asked. They're always present. For this modality, Ra-Ta or Cayce himself can be called upon. You can use the imagery you called on in the Ra-Ta guided initiation practice we did earlier or call in whomever you feel can best assist you.

Above all, I try to be open. Just the other day, a few guides I had not seen in a while showed up for my semicircle and I was happy they were there. When I say "see," of course I am talking about in my mind's eye, because I typically have my eyes closed for this process. If I haven't seen a particular guide in a while, I may say something like, "Oh wow! Great to see you!" I treat them in the same way as I would a treasured friend. Usually my group smiles and chats a bit, about what I cannot always say. It's all very cerebral in a sense and non-physical. Then everyone begins to settle down a bit, and I know that it's time to begin.

Most of the people I know in the spiritual community have their own set of guides, so call in your favorites, while being open to whoever else shows up. You'll likely get a pleasant surprise or two along the way.

4) Say a Prayer—Even though this session is for you, feel free to open your personal healing session with a prayer. Earlier in the book I gave the idea of prayer before my guides are called in, so when we get to the part where you try this yourself, just remember that I have my own ways of doing things, and you can also do this as you like. I have worked with my guides for so long now that I know them, and I simply expect they will show up when I call them. I am grateful for that knowledge. Once they're there, then I know that it's time to get started. Thus, I like to say a little prayer before we begin. With other modalities, such as Reiki, I always said:

"I thank my guides, angels, and ascended masters for being with me today. We surround this healing with love and light and ask that Higher Will be done."

Now that I am working specifically with the Edgar Cayce's Egyptian Energy Healing, or ECEEH, we have a beautiful prayer I included earlier in the book in the Prayer section that I really love to use with this modality due to its straightforwardness and because of the fact that Source says this should always be our prayer:

"THY WILL, O LORD, NOT MINE, BE DONE IN AND THROUGH ME."   2390-1

What more could we ask for than that when it comes to being open and receptive to healing? I love it, and I've decided to deem this the official opening prayer for the ECEEH method. Of course, we all know that Source said many amazing things along the same lines, so if you like something better, go for it; but for me, this is it—short, sweet, and to the point, with a wonderfully loving intention of helpfulness.

The other reason I love this prayer so much is that it humbly reminds us that as healers, or Light Bearers, we are not in charge. The healing energy comes through us because we have given our permission to be a channel, but it is not *of us*. We are not *causing* the healing; we are *facilitating* the transference of energy from ourselves to others. A wonderful reminder!

So once the guides are in place, I thank them for being with me and say my prayers; then I close my eyes, settle in, and prepare to begin sending the symbols to myself.

5) Envision Each of the Symbols—Keep the book by your side and refer to the photos of the symbols on page 187. Many times, I will keep my pictures by my side with other modalities so that I know I'm doing them correctly. Then again, once your spirit guides show up, they will ensure that the energy is conveyed properly for no other reason than because you set your intent for that to happen. So, while I do recommend you use your symbol pictures, you can also use your imagination to see the symbols however you personally envision them, or you could make a written list of only the names because that would also work. Once you have the intention of your symbols in place, you can begin sending them.

I recommend that you begin by sending each one of these symbols in the order Cayce and Source mentioned them. In all healing systems, symbols become more effective based on the order in which they are sent. I know from working with the Cayce life readings for so many years that Source is reliable and there is always a reason why certain things are said a particular way. There are no accidents, no coincidences. These symbols were given in this order for a reason, so honor that. Later we will discuss exceptions.

Now that Ra-Ta has officially initiated you, you'll start to feel the unique energies the symbols have once you begin working with them, and you will know which ones resonate best with you—which ones you need more of and which ones you can potentially do without. When you first begin though, it's a good idea to send all the symbols to yourself. With ECEEH it's important to start all the symbols off in your crown chakra center first because this initiates you, so to speak, into the energy system itself. If you've had a Reiki attunement, for example, you know that the Reiki Master passes energy to you by means of attunement. Because ECEEH is presented in this book in its entirety, the way you initiate yourself is through the crown chakra. Once that happens, the next time you work with the symbols, if you're like me, you may find yourself planning to send them through the crown but realizing that they behave differently.

Another important phenomenon to consider before beginning your healing is that when you send energy, it's like riding a wave on a surfboard. At first, there is no wave, and then the wave gets stronger, crashes into the shore, and fades away into nothing. Healing is exactly like an ocean wave. When you send a symbol, you feel nothing at first, and then the energy begins to flow and builds to a crescendo, after which it crashes down and ends. That's when you move on to the next symbol. Coming up later in this book, I included a Frequently Asked Questions section with further information on this concept. For now, know that you must follow your intuition on how long each symbol takes to send by feeling the waves of energy. With ECEEH in particular, I've noticed that the longer you work with the symbols and the more familiar your energy field becomes with the modality, the less time it takes to receive the benefit. While you're first working on yourself, take all the time you need and know that is perfect. Let's begin.

Lamp of the Light Bearers = Illumination

The Lamp is an incredible symbol for opening up to allow divine energy to come through. Remember that the symbol is always a representation of a subconscious intention, so in this case, for me, the Lamp signifies the ancient times in the Egyptian Temple when more experienced initiates worked diligently to assist their brothers and sisters in raising vibrational frequencies and transcending material reality. That's why I visualize the Lamp in my mind first, and by so doing, I energetically agree that the little picture of the Lamp in my mind represents all of those things. The Lamp represents, as Cayce would say, an *ideal*.

Once I worked with Lamp awhile, I began noticing that it illuminated the energy fields in and around the body, including the outer fields and seemed to set the tone for receiving all other energies, ultimately making the healing more successful.

When I first began working with Lamp, it took quite a while to allow it to do its work on me. Lamp really burns off unwanted energies and lower vibrations so your energy field can begin the journey of reaching new heights. Depending on all you've come here to learn, the transformation can take a while. Every time you do the session on yourself, you're likely to experience greater shifts in energy as the Lamp continues to shift your energy. Over time, you will really begin to sense the full potential Lamp contributes to illuminating your field. I imagined a commanding healer in the ancient times, some 10,500 years ago, helping me and sending me the energy. You may want to try that kind of visualization, but that's not necessary. The Lamp will do the work regardless.

When I send the Lamp, I begin by seeing the symbol in my mind's eye, or if I feel I need additional assistance, even I will refer to the drawings to remind myself how it is supposed to look. Once the symbol is firmly in my mind, I imagine seeing the Lamp hovering over my head, and then I begin sending it down through the crown of my head, imagining I can feel it move through my face, into each vertebrae of my neck, moving down into my shoulders, my arms, and slowly moving through my spine, into my legs, and down into the soles of my feet.

When I first used the Lamp symbol, there was a real opening that happened for me, especially through the head and into my shoulders. The energy continued flowing down my torso into my arms and legs. I believe the Lamp symbol sets the tone and opens the session similarly to unlocking a door to allow the light to flow in to the entire body. Some days, because I do this often, the Lamp hovers around my head, or I might feel it working more on my etheric bodies than on my internal energy system. When this happens, I allow it, and I don't try to force anything. Then I follow with each subsequent symbol, allowing the energy to flow as quickly or as slowly as needed.

The first time you do this, or perhaps the first several times, you may want to imagine Lamp moving through the whole body, so that all of your cells and energy fields are affected by it. Then once that has been established, you may find, as I did, that it hovers over certain areas, or perhaps simply stays above the crown chakra as an opener for the rest of the healing to begin.

Whenever you work with energy on yourself or others, by allowing yourself to pace each session based on energies you feel flowing out of your hands, or through your body, you send the right amount each time. There is a true ebb and flow of energy you'll feel or sense, and you will know when it's really flowing and when it stops.

When you send yourself the Lamp, picture the image of the Lamp entering the top of your head through your crown chakra center and feel the energy moving down your body toward the soles of your feet. Although that's the goal, you must still allow the energy to do what it will. Lamp might stay in your head area for a while, or you might feel a surge of electricity moving down the neck, into your shoulders and spine, and continuing into your arms and legs. Know that your time frame and process are perfect. Take as long as you need to allow the Lamp to move into every single cell of your body, ending in your feet. Lamp is a powerful symbol. If you're like me, you may initially feel a huge surge of energy. That buzzing feeling might last awhile, and then at some point, a few minutes later, or maybe quite a while later, that surge of energy will subside. That's when you know that it's time to move on. Good job!

Beetle = World

The scarab beetle symbol is next. Once the Lamp energy subsides, you can send the Beetle through the top of your head, through the crown chakra toward your feet.

I initially imagined the Beetle moving through my crown chakra, down my spine, and into my legs and feet. When I first worked with Beetle, I immediately realized the symbol is helpful in the third–eye chakra area. Beetle is vibrating at a violet purple frequency, so after passing the symbol through my field, the next time I sent this one to myself, I envisioned it as a large beetle placed directly over my face. I allowed the energy to permeate my entire head, and then I noticed that it began to vibrate downward through my spine. As this happened, I simultaneously felt the energy shoot up my left leg and into both feet, making its way toward the torso, where it spun around in my heart center. Very powerful!

My experience with Beetle shifted the second time I used it. So, follow the steps, but be open to possibilities. Once you let go of expectations and allow the energy to flow freely, then you will receive maximum benefit.

Be open to guidance and your amazing imagination. Notice where the energy pauses or stops altogether. Once Beetle moves completely through the body into all your cells and down your spine through the legs and feet, you may be guided to consciously place the Beetle directly over the third–eye chakra, which is where I believe it works best. Once you have the Beetle in place, patiently allow the symbol to work for you by feeling this energy tingle in the body for as long as you need. You might notice a warmth in the head or an expansion of energy around your upper body. Or not! As I will continue to remind you, there is no right or wrong in this and everyone is different. Just notice whatever you feel, and allow the sensation to continue until that stronger feeling subsides. Then move on.

Cockerel = Birth

When guided, move on to Cockerel. Again, the first time you do this, you will allow the image of the Cockerel symbol to move through your crown chakra and progress through the body to the feet. I know this sounds repetitious at times, but I am constantly reminded of the old saying, "Repetition is the mother of learning." Once you do your very first sessions with ECEEH, you may experience different sensations later on, but at least this first time, bring the symbol into the entire body. Then, as I've mentioned earlier, I often experience this symbol resting near the throat chakra. Allow it to go wherever you believe it is needed, and then notice how you feel. Pay attention to any sounds you hear, or colors, or other images you see. Allow Cockerel to work until it fades; then move on.

Earlier I mentioned that the Cockerel is helpful for opening the throat chakra. I figured this out initially because when I first began working with the Cockerel symbol, I heard the audible sound of *cock-a-doodle-doo*, like the sound of a rooster's crowing in the early morning. In a similar fashion to what happened with the Beetle, after my initial initiation and activation of sending the Cockerel through my crown chakra and down my body, the next time I used it the Cockerel symbol went straight to my throat before I could even try to send it through my crown chakra. I immediately sensed that it helps balance out the thyroid and other throat conditions. It also assists us in opening up our voice and speaking our truth. It is a symbol for the third chakra.

The cockerel's crow vibrationally clears out old stagnant energies and allows you to flow in your truth. I've found it to be truly powerful! The symbol blasted through my throat and began relaxing the muscles in my neck and throat. As the tension dissipated, I felt the energy push down into the shoulder blades, relaxing my upper back, and making my body feel a sense of deep relief and rest. This might be because I spend too much time at the computer—a problem plaguing our modern society. More than that though, it seems to really push away old blocks preventing communication and gives you a feeling of openness and peace. Try it yourself and see how you feel using this one.

Serpent = Mind

Next, imagine seeing the Serpent picture and send it in through your crown and move it down the body toward the soles of the feet. You might notice the Serpent branch off and move into the arms and hands, or it might move straight down the spine into the legs and go into the feet from there. Either way is okay as long as it moves through the whole body. Once the Serpent finishes round one, you may notice it moves upward again. Serpent may move up your spine, expanding your energy field, or it might settle near the base of the spine and spin for awhile before heading back toward your head. Notice what you notice. How does it feel or look to you? Continue to allow Serpent to work for as long as you need. You might find, as I have, that Serpent flows to the base of your spine and winds up toward your head, or not. It may release unwanted tension in your arms and legs. Or not. Allow and see what happens! If you've practiced Kundalini exercises before, you may notice the Serpent activates that energy as well. Either way, it's all good. Use your intuition and know all is well.

When I first started using ECEEH, I initially sent the Serpent symbol through my crown chakra and allowed it to move downward from there. Once that finished, the next time I worked with Serpent, the symbol swirled in snakelike fashion down to the base of my spine. I felt a strong jolt and then sensed the serpent spiraling upward, moving through my entire torso, until it returned to my crown chakra and moved downward again, this time with a more powerful circular motion. On the second pass down the spine, Serpent then continued on, shooting powerful energy through my legs, spiraling down through my thighs, knees, calves, and exited out the soles of my feet. Another "branch," so to speak, moved into my arms and shot out the tips of my fingers, energizing, enlivening, and rejuvenating my entire being.

Hawk = Wisdom

When you're ready and the Serpent energy has tapered off, send Hawk through the top of your head by imagining the picture coming into the crown, allowing it to flow through your body, pausing near your heart. Feel Hawk opening the heart chakra for as long as it takes and then continue to move down through your body, perhaps pausing, if needed, near the solar plexus chakra as it moves toward the legs and soles of your feet.

Once that's complete, you may sense the Hawk flying around you, enlivening your etheric fields of body, mind, and spirit. You may also imagine Hawk flying to other areas of the body. During various sessions, I've seen Hawk split up and become several smaller Hawks, and I've seen the Hawk become gigantic. Use your imagination and your connection with your personal spirit guides and helpers to help you envision Hawk in whatever form is for your highest good. Allow the wisdom of the Hawk to work as long as necessary. Notice what you notice, feel what you feel, and know all is well. Once the energy lessens, then move on.

The reason why I mention this varied imagery is because the first time I sent Hawk through my crown chakra, the symbol initiated me by traveling down through the base of the spine and through my arms and legs. The second time, I felt a blast of light in my crown before the Hawk flew downward toward my heart and seemed to settle in on my solar plexus area.

Cayce and Source said this symbol relates to Wisdom. Some say that the heart center is where the real brain is located. There's a lot of truth to that! Another reason is because of the school of thought about kinesthetic (feeling/ sensitive) people that says you get gut instincts and hunches in your solar plexus first, so some people believe your stomach/gut area houses a second brain. There's wisdom in all our cells in all parts of our body, so Hawk assists by awakening our divine wisdom for our highest good and potential.

When I first began using ECEEH with my clients, the sensation from Hawk so powerfully affected both my heart and solar plexus that I further perceived Hawk as more of a heart-healing symbol. I believe in the modern world our heart energy is often entangled in the power of the solar plexus region, and there must be balance and reverence given to the wisdom of the heart, or as Source said, the wisdom of the Hawk.

I was guided to draw the wing to look like half a heart and during my self-healing, the energy ultimately settled into my heart, spinning around and opening up that space. Hawk swirled around in a counterclockwise direction, opening the heart center which created a bright green light behind my eyelids. Hawk spins and heals, while turning back the wheels of time, like a fountain of youth. Very energizing!

I share these visual images with you so you will be open to what comes up after you first send the Hawk through your own crown chakra. Know that all the symbols are multidimensional and will help you in numerous, unpredictable ways.

Cross = Life

Once the Hawk is done fluttering around your energy field, go ahead and look at the Cross symbol and allow that image to move in through the crown of your head, speeding down your neck, into your arms and hands, moving down your spine and legs, and finally reaching your feet. Next, you may notice the Cross moving through your energy fields, going wherever it is most needed. This ancient power symbol might take awhile longer to work through your energy fields, especially the first time you use it, or not. Again, I cannot tell you exactly what will happen, just trust your own intuitive gifts and know that you are guided and supported in your efforts. However you experience the energy is perfect. I only mention the lengthier time in the energy moving through because I truly believe many of us guided to work with the Cayce material are reincarnated from ancient Egypt, and as such, the symbol activates unseen energies within you that can be quite profound. The Cross may linger in certain places, and if so, be open and allow.

Several of my clients really resonated with the Cross symbol when I worked on them. The ankh image really packs a punch. When I first brought it into my crown chakra, it took quite some time for it to work its way through my body and reveal how it is best used. As I began working with the Cross, I realized that once you bring the symbol through the crown and body, it should be drawn, or imagined, in subsequent healings over the solar plexus, where the crossline hits right in the area at the convergence of the rib cage. The circular top of the ankh should be imagined or drawn over the head and heart, as I did for myself in my own healing process. If you use your imagination to see the circular top of the ankh surrounding your heart, head, and shoulders, and the horizontal line crossing through your solar plexus at the top of your ribcage, then visualize the bottom line of the cross shooting down through the exact center of the physical body, grounding you to earth while illuminating you with light and love. That's how I experienced the ankh. It's as though this ankh is as big as you are and is placed right over your body. Very healing! I felt cells releasing and opening up for the purpose of receiving more light. The frequency of my entire energy body was rising. Know that you may be different though. So, while this is suggested, if Cross does something different when you use it, that's fine too.

I mentioned how Hawk wanted to be in both the heart and solar plexus areas, and I believe that the Cross symbol is similar because there is a healing that takes place in the core or center of the person which balances the heart energies with the ego–secular energies, bringing a more spiritual aspect to the life–force. However Cross shows up for you, continue to experience the energy until you feel it slow down, and then move on.

Crown = Power

Next glance at the picture for the Crown and send that symbol through the crown chakra, sensing the symbol traveling down your spine and through your entire physical body and energy field. Notice any sensations and take as long as you need. Once the Crown travels through your fields, you might find the Crown symbol turns back around once it reaches your feet and begins moving back up the body, splitting away from the body near the base of your spine, lifting and expanding your etheric bodies around your physical shell, or not. If so, you might imagine your outer fields of spiritual, mental and material, as Cayce called them, filling with new light and energy. Good job. When you're ready, move on to the next symbol.

The first time I imagined sending this simple V-shaped symbol through my crown chakra, I realized that it was more potent than I would have imagined. Quickly flashing down my spine, the Crown burst open the energy fields and then landed at the base of my spine, shooting into my arms, legs, and feet, and began fanning up toward the crown again. I concluded that this symbol works on the outer layers of our energetic field. The tips of the Crown burst into those outer fields and clear them of unwanted energies, which you will experience yourself later.

I was initially inclined to think of the Crown symbol as a sacral chakra opener, but the symbol never rests within the physical body and always aligns with the fields over and around the physical shell instead. Remember our earlier section in the book about the material, mental, and spiritual layers of the field? These always need to be cleared in an energy healing process, so know that the Crown works on those areas.

After my first experience, the Crown gave me a rush of energy at the base of my neck that shot up toward the head and opened up outer layers of my field in later sessions. To raise overall consciousness, you must work not only on physicality, but also on the etheric bodies as well, and this is what the Crown does best. Try it and see how you like it.

Gate/Door = Ascension

Experience the energy of the Gate/Door by allowing the image to move through the top of your head to the base of your spine. This is an especially strong symbol for most everyone I've worked with so far, and I believe you will find it to be powerful as well. Imagine that the Door/Gate symbol moves through the soles of the feet, then returns up to the base of your spine, where it blasts open your root chakra, grounding you to Mother Earth, stabalizing and energizing you. Feel that connection to Mother Earth as the Gate/Door moves into every cell, reminding you that although you are a spritual being, you are on this planet at this time for a reason.

I mentioned earlier that I took a little time figuring out what to use as the symbol for the Door/Gate and was guided to use the Egyptian hieroglyph for the Door to represent both of these items that Source mentioned.

From the moment I first sent this Door symbol down through my crown chakra, I found it to be the strongest of all the symbols. Maybe that is because the energy of the Door/Gate was exactly what I needed most—grounding. Door blasts open the root chakra and ties us to the earth. That's why we're here as human beings this time around—to be here and to have a physical experience in a body.

I've had periods in my life of being incredibly ungrounded, especially when I first started working as a healer. I have spent a lot of time working on myself over the years, and although I know I've gotten much better about being grounded than I used to be, I still find I need help in this area. Without grounding, we can't get anything done. We also long for other realms and daydream.

I've had clients needing this symbol more than ever these days too, and I think it's because of all our electronics and the fact that we are out in la-la land most of the time rather than being on the ground on our planet, living in our bodies. This is not good! We need to be connected to earth both for ourselves as physical beings and for the planet herself. How are we going to consciously make an impact to save our world from pollution and other threats if we're not willing to even be here? We need to disconnect from technological distractions and reconnect to earth and to each other now more than ever!

For me, Door has been amazing—a real game changer, and like all of these symbols, I feel the benefits increase over time the more I use the ECEEH.

So when you're sending this one, see how you feel and imagine that you can also benefit from the grounding energies Door/Gate provides. Allow yourself to ground to Mother Earth while preparing to access the higher realms of ascension, shifting frequencies to that of oneness and completion as you prepare for your final symbol. When you feel the process is complete, after allowing Gate/Door to move and go where it will, take note of various sensations, thoughts, and feelings. When you're ready, move on.

Way = Source

Envision the image of the Way symbol appearing over the top of your head. Allow the whole symbol to move into your head, neck, and shoulders, and then into your arms, down your spine, and into your legs until it reaches the soles of your feet. Take your time and allow the whole symbol to move where it needs to until you sense it has finished.

Next, put the symbol in your field using your imagination again to envision that the Lamp symbol is sitting above the top of your head and that the inverted Lamp (or bottom of the Way symbol) is coming up through the soles of your feet. You might perceive the Way symbol as a sparkling energy bubbling through your field quite quickly, removing blockages and making you feel energized. Notice the two Lamp symbols moving toward each other until they both reach your center or torso area, energizing your whole body and every single part of your energy field until you become so bright and bubbly that you sense yourself being surrounded by a wonderful ball of stunning, bright white light. Imagine that the ball of light surrounds you and moves within your body, healing you and spinning at an ultra high speed in the counter-clockwise direction. The beautiful white ball of light continues to spin faster and faster, relieving you of stress and enlivening your energy fields. The light gets brighter and brighter and brighter, lighter and lighter. Imagine that this incredible high-frequency light makes you feel loved, supported, and peaceful as you fully connect with Source energy. Know that you can carry this Source energy with you today and always, using it to bring you more peace and energy in your daily life, while at the same time, the white light serves as a protective shield so that only that which is of your highest good can come through.

To give you an idea of how this feels and what you might experience, I discovered the symbol for the Way after working with these energies and having visions of the Lamp symbol relighting itself at my crown chakra while a second Lamp symbol appeared and moved to the soles of the feet. Once the symbol for the Way was clear in my mind, I envisioned the entire symbol over my crown chakra and allowed it to move through my head, neck, shoulders, arms, spine, legs, and feet and blast into the ground. Next, a beautiful ball of stunning, bright white light appeared and illuminated my field. That light began swirling around quickly in a counterclockwise direction, and as my body sat inside this spinning light, I felt amazing and refreshed.

Allow the Way symbol to light up your field. Like putting the wrapping paper on a gift, the Way symbol seals your physical body and energetic self in a protective light.

With this new clearing and healing, know that you have a protective shield around you and that you have successfully set up balanced conditions within your energy fields and have surrounded yourself with loving, protective light from your Source or Creator. Go into the world as a mirror of love and light for those you encounter today. Great job!

***

I hope you enjoyed your experience with the ECEEH. You can practice whenever you feel guided. The more you do the process on yourself, the easier it will become. You will find that some symbols take longer to work. You may seem more drawn to them than others, while other symbols, after one single use, are not guiding you to work with them as much. After trying this a time or two, you may be able to move very quickly through the steps and do a rapid healing on yourself a few minutes in the morning or evening, depending on what suits you.

You may also want to take notes of things you experience by recording them in a healing journal. I am big on writing down experiences so I can remember how far I've come or know what areas need more work. I'd love to hear from you about any feedback you have on your healing journey and wish you well with this process. That's it for self-healing. Next up, we will look at how to use this with others.

Healing Others

Once you feel comfortable working on yourself using the ECEEH method, then you can pass Edgar Cayce's Egyptian Energy Healing to others by doing a session for someone. You will use the same guidelines that we've been covering so far. These days, many of my sessions are done via distance healing which we will discuss in a little while, but when I do in-person sessions, they are either on a massage table or while the person is sitting in a chair. Either way works, depending on the tools you have at your disposal. Here are the steps:

1) **Set the Space Accordingly**—Using guidelines mentioned before, set your sacred space however you choose. Depending on your situation, you might find yourself working with people on a massage table or in a chair. I used to always use my massage table when working on people until I started doing more public healings in expos and fairs. Then I found the table to be cumbersome and realized that it's just as effective to have your recipients sitting in a chair. That is particularly true with ECEEH, since your goal is to send the energy through the crown of their head, so that is easily done when your clients are sitting down. Either way is fine depending on your preference. Set the tone of the session by putting on music, adding essential oils if the clients are not allergic to them, amplifying the energy using your favorite gems and stones . . . whatever makes you feel grounded, open, and prepared. If you're in your own office space, of course, you can have the room set up as you want, but if you go out to psychic fairs and expos, you need to be aware that you may have to be flexible with your space and say a prayer before you begin to set the tone for your session and day as a whole.

2) **Prepare Yourself**—Clean your hands and before you start or before the person arrives. Also, you would greatly benefit from sitting quietly and imagining yourself receiving all of the symbols, in order, coming through the crown chakra, down the spine and into all the other areas of the body, arms, hands, legs, and feet. Imagine you are attuning yourself to the energy so you can be the best channel possible for ECEEH .

3) **Greet Your Clients and Do Discovery**—However you feel best you will greet your clients and find out how they're doing, what they would like assistance with, and if they enjoy working with any particular guides or angels. You might be working on your best friends in the world and know everything there is to know about them, which is great, but even so, ask a few questions here because you might learn something new! You could also be doing a healing for clients whom

you don't know very well, in which case, it's always good to chat a little before beginning to get to know them better.

Here are a few questions you might consider:

1) Have you ever had energy healing before?

2) If so, what kind?

3) What are you working on now that I can assist you with?

As always, use your intuition! Once they're settled in, then you're ready to begin.

4) Recite a Prayer—

"THY WILL, O LORD, NOT MINE, BE DONE IN AND THROUGH ME."   2390-1

I begin the session with the Cayce prayer listed above. You should find out if the person receiving the healing is okay with you saying all of this aloud or not. Normally I say this to myself.

5) Call in Guides, Angels, or Ascended Masters –I always invite my own guides to help me in any healing. Typically, I do this silently. When you work with other people, if you'd like and if it feels appropriate after speaking with them, you can invite their unseen helpers in by also saying something like:

"We ask that John's (or whatever the name is) guides and ascended masters join us today as we do this healing, and we know that only that, which is of Highest Good, can come through. May Higher Will be done."

You may also choose another prayer if you prefer. Here's a version of the one I mentioned earlier:

"John and I thank our guides, angels, and ascended masters for being with us today. We surround this healing with love and light and ask that Higher Will be done."

Then, right before I begin, I might also add:

"I thank my guides, angels, and ascended masters for being with me today. We surround this healing with love and light and ask that Higher Will be done."

Earlier in the book, we discussed the goal for prayer and the importance of setting intentions. The main objective is to declare your well wishes for the recipients of your healing energies. You want to imagine them as healthy, happy, and filled with love and light, so remember that the words don't matter. No matter what words you say, healing is your purpose. Now that the stage has been set, so to speak, you're ready to begin sending symbols.

6) Begin by Sending All Symbols—Remember, there's nothing wrong with referring to your photos, so if you'd like, please refer to page 187 and have the symbols out when you begin your session.

When I first work with people, just as when I used ECEEH on myself, I must begin at the crown of the head and envision the Lamp symbol moving in through the top of their head. I then use my hands to bring the symbol down through the neck and shoulders, arms, hands, legs, and feet. I may pause along the way depending on what's happening. Extra healing is often needed in certain areas, so I allow this to go on as long as it is needed.

Beetle = World

Next, I bring Beetle through the top of the head, moving toward the feet for as long as it takes. Once that's done, with some people I saw the Beetle illuminate in purple over the third-eye area, but not always. Use your intuition to see what is best and what resonates.

Cockerel = Birth

Cockerel is next so go ahead and bring that symbol through the crown of the head and allow it to move as it will down the body. Similar to Beetle, once the Cockerel has moved through the field, it progressed to the throat area with some clients, while other times it simply floated into the field bringing a sense of personal power. Any healing process involves some element of imagination and listening to guidance in terms of where the symbol goes and what it does for the recipient. Trust yourself and your guides and go with what you believe is best.

Serpent = Mind

Next, send the Serpent through the crown and down the spine. I always see this one as spiraling around the spine as it makes its way to the feet. Every single time I have worked with Serpent, I find that once it has hit the client's feet, it spirals back upward toward the head again and breaks off, sometimes into several serpents that slither down the arms and legs, enlivening the energy fields while waking the dormant Kundalini serpent energy that resides at the base of the spine.

For some of my clients, this sensation was stronger than for others. I simply follow my inner impressions and go from there. Use your inner vision, knowing that your unseen guides and helpers are assisting you in every step of the process.

Hawk = Wisdom

Send Hawk through the crown. You may find Hawk will fly through the head, stop and spin around the heart and solar plexus for a while, as mentioned earlier, or perhaps not. Be open. Just notice Hawk and allow the energy to eventually make its way to the feet. Some clients were like me and had the Hawk hover over the solar plexus region, while others had Hawk fluttering around the exterior fields around the body. Once the Hawk makes its way through the crown chakra, allow it to go where it needs. You may also want to think about the word and the spirit of *wisdom*—the wisdom of the body to heal itself, to realign in a state of perfection while visualizing the client feeling well and healed. Allow the Hawk to work until that energy subsides.

Cross = Life

Beginning from the crown, allow the Cross to move down the spine, potentially pausing along the way near the center of the body, before arriving at the feet. Allow the Cross to linger for as long as necessary. Take your time seeing the life of the Cross symbol illuminating the clients' dormant life–force, giving them renewed vitality and energy. When I did this, I had very clear perceptions of which clients had past lives in Egypt. You may notice this as well, and if you do, you may want to pass that information on to them after the session is over.

Crown = Power

The Crown will begin at the crown chakra, move down the body and to the feet, but then I allow it to go ahead and expand into those outer layers of body, mind, and spirit, strengthening the energy fields and healing everything. Crown often causes the temperature of the other person to chill down as the frequencies rise. I had this happen several times. When you shift the wavelengths of energy around a person to higher dimensions, the air is a bit chilly, which told me the process worked wonderfully.

Gate/Door = Ascension

Next, send the Gate/Door. You may notice how it blasts through the crown, moving toward the feet. Imagine while Gate/Door shoots toward the base of the spine, it begins to illuminate the legs and arms as well. When the frequencies of the energy rise dramatically, you may notice a tangible chilly feeling around the client's body. This happens when energy frequencies rise. The higher the vibration becomes, the cooler the air. Notice how the cool air intensifies at times as the lower energies are long gone, and the person accepts a higher frequency of energy into their light bodies.

Way = Source

Finally, envision the Way symbol in full at the crown of the head and imagine that it moves through the entire body. Remember, I won't move the full symbol over the soles of the feet and crown again until a bit later when I am ready to end the session.

7) Continue Your Healing by Following Intuitive Guidance

From here, after all the symbols have been introduced into the person's energy field, I let my guides take over and I allow myself to move to any areas of the body where I believe the person needs healing.

If you've worked in healing in the past, you know that for no logical reason at all you may be guided to move to different areas of the body and linger there. While there, I may, for example, see Hawk in my mind as I stand near the heart. I envision the heart center opening fully; I see the person in amazing health—vital and vibrant as Hawk enlivens that area. Beetle may hover over the recipient's forehead, or the Crown might move in the outer layers of the field. Serpent might move up and down the spine several times before a real shift in energy happens. Whatever the guidance tells me to do, I do it.

I also know that with my guides and helpers whom I called in earlier, they will help me ensure the healing is a success. What that means would vary from person to person. What you need, for example, isn't what your neighbor needs. At times, I may not know what the person is going to do with the energy; I only know I was guided to send it in the order or way that I did.

Also notice that with each symbol you send, there is a rise and fall of energy. Pay attention to when the energy gets stronger and when it begins to taper off. When that happens, know that you can move on to the next area of the body that needs attention. During this quiet time, do you receive any messages for the person? Did you have any flashes of insight? If so, what? Are these insights things you will pass on to the person, or were the messages more for your personal benefit so you could better assist the recipient during the healing session? Some people want to hear messages you receive, others do not, so if you feel like you received something important, ask the recipients if they'd like to hear insights and then honor their wishes on whether that information would be welcomed or not. Continue this part of your session for as long as needed.

8) The Way and Ball of Light—Once you feel you're done, it is now time to finish up sending the Way by placing the Lamp image over the crown chakra and the inverted version of the Lamp into the soles of their feet. Imagine the client's energy field enlivened and envision the person surrounded by a twinkling white light of protection that becomes brighter and brighter, lighter and lighter, and begins spinning in a counterclockwise direction. Once the two Lamps are in place, know that the work is done and that the field is set with a new, higher frequency.

9) End in Prayer—End your session by bringing the hands to the prayer position. Why? Because when your hands are flowing with energy, they are like circuits. To bring the energy transference to an end, you must close the circuit by pressing the tips of the fingers together. Additionally, when you bring your hands into the prayer position, you can actually strengthen your energy fields around your body. You are collecting any scattered energies and telling your Higher Self to strengthen your energy field by shielding you from unwanted influences.

In the case of healing sessions, hopefully you had enough time to work on the person, so the energy should stop flowing on its own, or at least dwindle down a bit before your session ends. Still, it is an important gesture for any healing work because you want to send bright blessings to all you serve. Once that is complete and your hands are in a prayer position, recite or silently say the Cayce prayer at the beginning of the session:

> "THY WILL, O LORD, NOT MINE, BE DONE IN AND
> THROUGH ME."   2390-1

Once you do that, you may also want to say other helpful words of your choice, or you can always use my other favorite intention for continual wellbeing:

> *"Please allow this healing to continue. May Higher Will be done."*

That's it! You've completed your session. Nice work!

***

You might want to ask the recipients for feedback on what they felt and how the energy flowed for them. Ascertain if they have any questions and if they would like another session in the future. And that's it! You did it! Good job!

How to Do Distance Healing for Others

Now that you've tried Edgar Cayce's Egyptian Energy Healing on yourself and hopefully had a chance to try it on someone who came by to visit you, let's talk next about how you are going to send someone the energy from a distance.

Distance healing is done the same way as you do any other healing. Because the recipient is off in the distance, I always sit in a comfortable place that is quiet and where I know I won't be disturbed. I begin to visualize the person in my mind. There are many ways to do this. I may have a photograph of the person, or I sometimes know the person. Most of the time, I don't have any idea what the recipient looks like, but that doesn't matter. Regardless of circumstances, once I set my intent to offer a healing, the work will be done.

In some ways, I find distance healing to be easier because I can simply tune in and get to the heart of the matter without having to worry about whether the person got stuck in traffic or got turned around and lost trying to find my office. That said, just because someone isn't sitting right in front of you doesn't mean that you can consider the session as anything but sacred. The distance healing should be treated with the same respect as the in-person session.

You still need to prepare yourself and your space and follow the same steps. Talking up front may take place over the phone or by email instead of in-person, but it's still important.

Let's look at the steps for your distance healing:

1) Fact Finding and Discovery—Unlike the in-person session, here you will want to either email the clients or talk to them on the phone about what they want to work on during their healing session. Perhaps they just need an energy boost, or there might be something more specific. Find out ahead of time, and you may want to ask what time of day they prefer receiving healing. I know some of my clients prefer evenings, some like mornings so they can be more supercharged for their day, while others like a relaxing zap before they go to bed at night. Everybody's different, so ask. You may also find the recipients prefer evening healings, but you are free only in the morning. If that's the case, fine. All you have to do is sit and follow these steps, adding the intention that the session be downloaded to them during their next sleeping cycle and know that it is done. Again, your guides will ensure this is handled as long as your intention is there.

2) Prepare Yourself and Your Space—Distance healings can be nice because typically you're in your own surroundings. Make sure you're comfortable and your space is how you want it, even though nobody will actually see you. Bring the ECEEH symbols through your system by envisioning all of them in order and sit in meditation to prepare before you begin. I sit quietly in my special meditation space, close my eyes, and clear out my own field. For ECEEH, I often use the Lamp symbol and imagine that it is burning brightly through my field, removing any unwanted influences, clearing me to receive the proper information for my clients. I may also send myself all of the symbols before working with clients, depending on how much time I have, or what I'm guided to do.

3) Prayer—Go ahead and recite the prayer, either to yourself or aloud—whichever you prefer. Remember, we are still set on seeing the people as healed, joyous, and happy.

"THY WILL, O LORD, NOT MINE, BE DONE IN AND THROUGH ME."   2390-1

Once I do that, I like to sit for a moment until I feel a sense of new energy come over me. It is like a subtle shift in my field which signifies that I am ready to begin.

4) Call in Guides, Angels, or Ascended Masters —Next, enlist the help of your guides. If you'd like and if it feels appropriate after speaking to your clients, you can also invite their guides in by saying something like:

"We ask that John's (or whatever the name is) guides and ascended masters join us today as we do this healing and we know that only that, which is of Highest Good, can come through. May Higher Will be done."

You can say this aloud or to yourself. Then once you sense that the guides have arrived, continue with:

"I thank my guides, angels, and ascended masters for being with me today. We surround this healing with love and light and ask that Higher Will be done."

5) Envision the Clients in Your Mind's Eye—Next, sit in meditation and begin to visualize the people you want to work on. If you don't know what they look like, just imagine that you can sense their energy. Knowing what they actually look like is not necessary at all. You are interested in the unseen energetic part of your clients. I also recommend allowing your guides to assist you with this visualization and show you how the people would best receive the healing.

There are two ways to handle this depending on what you are guided to do:

1) Imagine the recipients sitting in front of you. Envision the backs of their heads and imagine that you are standing behind them. Place their heads in your hands as you send symbols through the crown chakra. Cup your hands and imagine each image of each symbol moving in order down through their head and spine and into their legs and feet.

2) You could also do my other favorite strategy by imagining that their entire bodies are teeny tiny—so small that they fit in the palm of your hand. As a result, you can easily send each symbol to the entire body at once.

6) Send the Symbols in Order—Send all the symbols to your clients from head to toe. Take your time with each, noticing what symbols resonate best with the individuals. Continue sending each one until you feel that shift in energy. See page 187 for your symbol list if you'd like to refer to them during your session.

Begin with the Lamp. On the distance healing, you may notice an extra charge of energy when you send Lamp because this symbol opens the session and basically clears the channels of communication between your intention and the receivers no matter how far away they are. In Reiki one of its healing symbols opens people up to being able to receive distance healing, and in ECEEH the Lamp is used for this purpose. Pay attention to what you notice as the Lamp moves through the entire body toward the feet.

Next, send all of the other symbols in order, and since you're working on your own, it is fine to refer to the pictures. Nobody can see you, so go for it! By now you know what each will do, so use your intuition and see what happens. If you'd like, follow the steps from one of the earlier sections, or follow what you're guided to do. Once you send all of the symbols, remember that when you reach the Way symbol, place the entire image into the top of the head, allowing it to travel through the body.

Next, you'll allow any other insights to come in terms of which symbols need to go where. When I do the distance healings, I often sit and simply feel my hands tingling as the energy is transferring, and at times I may or may not know which symbol is being sent. I trust that the people are receiving what they need.

When you feel all residual healing is completed and there is a tangible sense that the energy flow is not as strong as before, visualize the Way again using the Lamp symbol over the crown chakra and the inverted Lamp over the soles of the feet with the twinkling white light of protection that begins spinning in a counterclockwise direction. Allow that light to amplify the energy bodies for as long as you need. I know I mention that final step a lot, and I'm doing it again here because the key to the whole system lies in that final step when you spin the field. Without that, it would be like baking a cake without putting any icing on top.

7) End in Prayer—Once you've sent the field spinning, wait until the energy begins to taper off a bit and you sense that the healing is complete. When this happens, bring your hands together to close the energetic circuit and say:

"Please allow this healing to continue. May Higher Will be done."

Remember that during this whole time I may or may not be seeing the people in my mind. I could have spent the whole time imagining their heads in front of me or their teeny bodies on a massage table, or perhaps I am holding up only my hands in the air and feeling the energy as it's being sent. I always do whatever I am guided.

8) Make a Note of Messages—Did you receive insights you need or want to pass on to the clients? If so, make a note and contact them afterward if they have expressed an interest in hearing the information.

***

Good job! How did you like that process? You will likely find, as I have, that these days most of my healing sessions are done at a distance. Taking notes about insights you receive during your sessions will surely assist future clients. That's it! The most important part is to have fun, see the best outcome for all you serve, and allow the universe to handle the details, knowing that all is well.

Group Healing

ECEEH works wonderfully in a group setting, following many of the same steps you use in your own self-healing session or individual sessions with other people.

The best example of Group Healing is a Reiki share. If you've ever participated in Reiki or another healing group, the primary goal is to have everybody take turns giving and receiving healing. The group energy gives you a chance to really experience the consciousness of how healing works. You get a feel for when the session should begin and when it should end. When I attend these sessions, the whole group works on someone. The space always seems quiet and serene as everyone collectively tunes in to the person on the table.

Miraculously, even though most of the healers may have their eyes closed or are one hundred percent focused on the person receiving the energy, somehow, at the same moment, group members physically step back and put their hands in prayer practically in unison, as if tuning into the divine as a collective unit. Have you seen this happen before? Anyone who has been healing for any period of time has surely seen what I am talking about. No matter how many years I work in the healing arts, I still find this incredibly interesting, because this demonstrates how we healers can collectively tune in to the higher wisdom of the soul without having to say a word.

Group healing is valuable because you won't get this kind of feedback working alone. You may sense it's time to end a session, but that immediacy of working with other people allows you to receive more easily visual and intuitive confirmation that the healing is complete.

Likewise, all the healers seem to naturally know where the recipient needs the most help. Everyone is silent with many having their eyes closed, and yet somehow you may be drawn to work on the person's leg and simply stay there, for example. It's an unspoken wisdom that rises up and is especially apparent at these times. Your hands go where they're needed, and there is not much conscious thinking involved at all. In fact, healing is one endeavor where thinking is not ideal!

The validation comes when the recipient is finished with the healing and often tells you, "My leg needed energy and now it feels better." How did you know that? It consists of consciousness and wisdom—the levels of understanding that are beyond our human selves. The group setting gives you an opportunity to really feel the divine nature of your healing abilities and to receive the validation you need to ultimately learn to trust yourself. Know that there's a reason for the intuitive insights and supposed random thoughts that may float in during healing sessions.

Unlike the individual healing sessions, when you work with a group, things are much more fluid and unpredictable. You may not follow the steps as you've done when working individually, and you may find that you must rely more on your intuition in terms of what the person receiving needs, as well as tuning in to the entire group's process and method.

To do Edgar Cayce's Egyptian Energy Healing with a group, you will divide up depending on how many people and massage tables you have, and take turns receiving the energy. Let's cover the steps.

1) Setting the Space and Preparing Your Energy—I assume that you have been invited to a space that has already been prepared, and if you're working with other people who are doing the ECEEH technique, hopefully they've had a chance to work with this modality themselves. Even if you're at a Reiki share or doing another modality, you can always allow other healers to use their resources or modalities and you can use the ECEEH if you are so guided.

2) Saying the Prayer/Calling in Assistance—In the Group Healing, it's nice if one person can go ahead and say a prayer aloud because everyone who attends knows that a healing is taking place, and as a result, folks are usually open to an auditory prayer. When I teach Reiki and other modalities, I usually say the prayer we've been doing all along:

"We ask that that Higher Will be done."

If you are with a group of like minds all doing the Edgar Cayce's Egyptian Energy Healing and are familiar with the processes, then you can go ahead with the Cayce prayer:

"THY WILL, O LORD, NOT MINE, BE DONE IN AND
THROUGH ME."   2390-1

If your friends aren't familiar with ECEEH yet, you might want to share that prayer with them. I've shared it with people, and everyone has a truly positive feeling from the loving intent of the words.

3) Move around the Person Receiving—Normally in a group, we do not have time for lengthy discussions on what the person is going through, or what the benefit might be, but once in a while someone might mention a sore shoulder, for example, and then of course, you can honor that by attempting to assist.

When I am teaching a class, I like to have someone from the group start at the head and someone else at the feet. Every time a session is over and we switch to the next person, I have people move around the table so that everyone gets to experience what it's like working on the head and feet and all other areas. That way, during the session, healers get much needed practice, which is what the group experience is all about.

Since there is an order to things in terms of the symbols, and let's say you're standing near the person's left shoulder, you could go ahead and just send the symbols to the person in order and allow them to travel where needed. Or you could begin with the Lamp symbol to open the energy and then allow your subconscious mind and Higher Self to let you know which of the other symbols is needed.

Having the group together makes this more of an intuitive experience for everybody because you cannot do the method in the same way as you do for yourself or for one solitary person. Be open to receive and enjoy the process.

Still to the best of your ability, I would recommend going through each symbol in order and sending it to the person wherever you happen to be. If every healer gets a chance to change positions, then everyone will benefit from experiencing how the energy works in terms of beginning a session with Lamp in the crown of the head and ending with the Way symbol moving through the soles of the feet, allowing the healer to experience the powerful new energy of the white light swirling around the person in a counterclockwise direction.

So be open minded to what comes, but for reference, please refer to page 187 to see your symbols again. Send all your symbols in order and do your best while the other healers are doing their work. The collective energy of having the whole group focus its intent on one person at a time means the group sessions are much shorter and are often only a few minutes long for each recipient, depending on how many people you have in your healing group.

So, what if you are busy sending away, and you're about to send the recipients the Gate/Door, when, all of a sudden, Hawk comes flying out of nowhere or Serpent slithers up their legs? Then go with it and know that is what's needed!

I offer guidelines to follow here for reference, but please know that if you and I meet in a class at some future time, I will impress upon you the fact that the Light Bearer, aka healer, aka you, must always do as guided at the time. That guidance supersedes any prior instruction. You've got this! Believe me, and even if you don't think you do, know that your guides have your back and that all is well.

4) End the Healing—Wait until the collective consciousness of the group senses the healing session is done, and then back away as a unit. How will you know when or how to do this? Amazingly, as I mentioned earlier, it just happens. The healers are usually doing their work, sending energy. Some have their eyes closed, appearing to be very far away from the present moment. Then, all of a sudden, the energy flow comes to an abrupt halt and everybody backs away. There is a tangible sense of energy coming to a halt, and the flow is done. It is like turning off the faucet or a hose. You will know when that happens.

5) End in Prayer—As you did before when working on one person, all the healers in the group should bring their hands to prayer position, closing the energetic circuit. Say aloud or to yourselves:

"Please allow this healing to continue, may Higher Will be done."
Visualize that the recipients are healthy, happy, and at their optimal energy.

6) Debriefing—Then allow the recipients to get up or help them as they might feel lightheaded. You may take a moment to share any intuitive insights you discovered while working on them. At times this is tough to do if you have a huge group, so just do your best. I like to do this though, if even briefly, because a lot of times everybody is getting the same exact information about the person, and if you're still working on building up your confidence as a healer, you can gain a lot from sharing this information. Sometimes we tend to brush off our insights as nonsense, but if three or four other people came up with the same "silly" idea as you did, then maybe it's time to take yourself more seriously and trust what you receive.

7) Switch to the Next Person—Allow the next person to go and repeat the steps and continue on until everyone has received a session.

8) Discussion and Closing—Time permitting and if you'd like, you can all sit afterward for shared insights and reflection on what you experienced. I think the sharing of experience is important because it helps the healers know that the things they felt, or saw, were not strange when they find out that other people had the same thing happen to them. Sharing is quite validating and can be truly educational. That's it! Fun and simple!

Other Fun Ways to Work with ECEEH

Aside from the typical ways to do energy healing, here are two more ideas for how you can get creative with ECEEH.

Charging a Crystal with ECEEH Energy

If you enjoy crystals as much as I do, another way you can effectively work with healing symbols and energy is to charge crystals with these vibrations. How does this happen? By pretending you're working on someone and sending the entire ECEEH modality into your crystal, one symbol at a time. This is the same thing as programming a crystal, only in this case, you are programming the crystal with ECEEH. I recommend sending the symbols in order in the same exact way you would send them to yourself or anyone else to achieve best results. Here are a few steps you can follow, and if you need to glance at the pictures of the symbols while you're working, that's great, refer to page 187:

1) Hold the crystal or gemstone in your hand.

2) Send each symbol into the stone, imagining each symbol being infused into your crystal for eternity to aid in your healing from that moment forward.

3) Take your time. Notice what you notice. Once you finish your programming, know that your crystal is ready to use now.

4) Carry your crystal around with you to benefit from those healing vibrations all day long.

I programmed one of my favorite crystal points with the ECEEH and believe me, this works! I've been carrying mine for the better part of a year now and from time to time, I've found it reminds me to reattune myself to ECEEH and to spin my energy field in the counterclockwise direction. The result is more energy for me to enjoy, and I hope you'll find the same.

To do this, I suggest looking at the symbols, at least the first few times you try it, and then send them one by one into the crystal. Imagine, for example, the picture of the Lamp, Beetle, Cockerel, and so forth being imbedded in your stone.

You will probably feel your hands heat up when you do this, so wait until they cool off; then know that you've successfully programmed your stone and you can carry it with you to benefit from the energies throughout the day.

Charging Water with ECEEH

Likewise, we can also get filtered water just as I showed you in the section on how to work with color-charged water, but instead of sitting a bright blue bottle in the sun for a period of time, you follow these steps:

1) Place filtered water into a glass container.

2) Place your hands over the jar.

3) Send each symbol in the correct order into the water. Please refer to page 187 to see the photos of the symbols.

4) Allow each symbol to flow into the water for as long as it needs. Feel and notice when it is flowing, and when it's time to move on to the next.

5) Enjoy the water and feel the helpful vibrations energize you for the day!

Frequently Asked Questions

Here is a brief list of some of the common questions I've been asked about Edgar Cayce's Egyptian Energy Healing. Enjoy!

Earlier you said the room became cold because of shifting vibrations. What does that mean?

Over the years, I've noticed that sometimes when energy shifts around the person, if the frequency is high enough, it can sometimes cause a sensation of a cool breeze or chill in the air around the person. Why that happens, I believe, is because cooler air has a higher frequency—a shorter wavelength. You can sometimes feel that, especially when someone is making a huge shift to a higher vibration or letting go of denser energy.

If someone wanted a healing in the evening, but you did the actual session earlier in the morning, would that work? If so, how?

Through the power of your intention, you can program this information for future download, similar to how you might request a software update on a computer system to run while you sleep. You simply go through the motions of doing the session in its entirety during the morning, or even the day before, and then at the end simply state your intention that either:

"I ask that this healing be downloaded and received at a time that is best for all concerned."

or

"Please allow this healing to be given this evening when John is alseep so by the following morning, he will be fully integrated into this new energy and information."

The first option makes the receiving more open ended with a stated caviat that as Light Bearer/Healer, I do not know the Higher Self of the recipient or the intention well enough to judge what that best time would be to receive a healing. I really like the idea of putting the highest and best out to the Universal Manager. The second option is more specific by listing the state of being that the client would be in when he receives the healing. I would not want to say this healing will be arriving at 9:00 p.m. Eastern Standard Time, for example, because what if John decides to stay up until midnight? That's none of my business, so instead I simply ask he receive the energy during the next sleep cycle.

Theoretically, this kind of preprogramming should seem somewhat rare or random, but as a healer, you would be surprised how often I do things like this for various reasons. Usually this comes up in classes where I am activating someone into the energy. If I teach Reiki, for example, and I initiate the student into all three of the healing symbols, I may sense that the student is not energetically ready to receive them all at once. I imagine I am setting the symbol in the student's etheric field so that it can be downloaded (there's that word again) at a later time.

With ECEEH, that's definitely possible, for sure. I know, because it actually happened to me. I had one client who did not seem to be energetically ready to receive the distance healing when I tried sending energy. I could have simply given up and said, "Oh well," but instead I imagined each of the symbols stacking up, one on top of the other, in the energy bodies in the person's etheric field above the crown chakra and asked the person's guides to gently deliver them at a later time. It is kind of like the holographic universe. I placed the thought of the symbols there, holographically using my imagination and knowing thoughts really are things; I knew for sure that they would be successfully received and used later at the optimal time for the client in question.

To me, this is like one of those annoying software downloads for your operating system. You've been alerted it's there, waiting, and you want to receive it, but you can't at the moment. It may be that there's a pressing issue keeping you from it. So how do you work around this? By simply telling your computer, aka in this case your Higher Self, to download the update in an hour, a day, etc. This is particularly useful these days because as always our vibrational frequencies around earth are in continual flux. Our light bodies need these energy downloads, believe me, so it's far better to do it slowly than not at all.

Again, I don't do this too often, but the strategy can come in handy if you don't feel a lot of energy when you send someone a particular symbol, just ask that the energy be put in the person's field until it's needed. It works!

Does that mean you would have to send them all of the symbols?

Maybe or maybe not. The other thing that happens is the recipient might receive all of the symbols except for one or two. How you will know is if you never have a sense of the symbol leaving the crown area of the head. It would simply float there and stay put. The ECEEH system is super dynamic, and I've found these symbols will blast down the spine normally. So if you find one that's sitting there, not going any-where, you may intuit to go ahead and move on to the next symbol for now, but know that the client may need to receive that symbol later. So let one or two of the symbols sit in the field on reserve until it's needed. When that happens, simply ask your guides and the client's Higher Self to make those symbols available whenever it is for the client's highest good, then move on and accept that the healing is finished and will be completed at the right time.

What if they don't seem to need a symbol and I don't feel that they will ever need the symbol?

If a symbol is floating there, not doing anything, and you've asked but feel guided that the person does not need this particular symbol, then set an intention that the energy is there for the person at any time in the future if needed. The client is free to accept or reject that energy and Higher Will be done. Once that's said, move on and let it go. I've found that when clients make huge vibrational shifts, it's not that they don't need the symbol, but they may literally not be able to integrate the symbol into their field at that moment. I always teach my students that you can never give people too much energy. Why? Because if it does not resonate with them, they will not accept it, and because you and I as healers are not in charge. Trust that they will get the healing if and when it's needed; then let go and let God.

You mentioned Cord Cutting. What is that?

There are invisible cords of light that connect you with other things and people. One of the best ways to release unwanted energy is to imagine these cords in your mind's eye and cut them, thereby freeing energy and blessing everyone. It's powerful!

You made this statement: "At times, healing can build upon itself and actually improve conditions over time, long after the person receives the energy." What did you mean by that?

We've been talking about energy fields throughout the book, and I mentioned that the field is infinite. The spiritual layer is in the outer part of the field, then comes the mental while the material is closest to the body. When you clear out those fields, the person feels better immediately; then over time as the cleared waves travel toward the body for the next hours and days, the vibration of good intentions you sent can actually feel expanded as time goes by. Like waves crashing on the shores of the soul, the healing is a gift that keeps on giving with increasingly wonderful results.

How often should you send the ECEEH to yourself or others?

As with all things, I would use this whenever you are guided. I work with this every day, and I have felt exponentially better and better over time. My fields are opening up and expanding in new ways with every use. When I have worked with other people, I noticed immediate shifts and changes in their energy while the system seems to build on itself over time. There is no right answer to this. That said, I do know that taking time to do energy healing has amazing benefits and helps you so your field remains clear and continually expansive over time. That translates into the outer world in numerous ways that are different for everyone. For you, that might mean you work with this every evening before drifting off to sleep, or in the morning as a meditation before heading out the door to work. Again, there is no right answer for this.

We talked a lot about programming. You could also ask your guides to provide you with an ECEEH session while you sleep and help you gently shift your frequencies in that way so it would not even take up real waking time, but you could still receive the benefits.

I'm a busy person. How much time are we talking about here?

That can vary. Again, the first time or two when I first do a session on someone, or even on myself, it takes longer to get used to the dynamic shifts in energy. Within two or three times, it shouldn't take long at all—often less than ten minutes to give yourself a tune up and quickly send all the symbols into the field. Each time you do the process, your field shifts into the higher frequencies and takes less of your time, but again, if time is a challenge, I'd ask my guides to help me out with either a morning tune-up right before I get out of bed to begin my day, or while I am sound asleep at night.

Yeah, but that sounds like a lot! Can't I give myself too much energy?

No. As discussed in the holographic explanation above, if you don't need it, you don't feel it; then the energy will sit until you do, or it may not do anything at all.

Why do you begin by sending energy through the crown chakra?

Awesome question! I have been passing attunements, also called activations or initiations, into healing modalities for many years now, and what I find is that if you send the healing symbol through the crown chakra, at least at first, it gives that symbol the chance to move down through the light bodies into the entire body, every single cell and nerve, where it can be best integrated into the whole. I often like to imagine the energy moving from the top of my head to the tip of my toes, and then once that's done, it can go work on whatever area it wants to. Usually I reserve this for myself, but I've also found when working on clients that when I send it through the crown first, rather than prejudging where I think it needs to be sent based on what other people experienced, I am then allowing for my intuition to go to work. My guides and angels send the vibrations to where that particular person needs it most, and I might not always know the correct place-ment. I may think I do, but anytime you're doing healing, you have to be prepared for the unexpected to happen and know that yes, we are all one, but we are also different and to be the best healer you can be, you must be open to the impulses coming in from the divine in order to best serve people.

Unlike other healing methods where you must take a course to receive the activation, by passing the energy through your crown and moving the vibrations through your body, you will self-attune and self-initiate into the energy so you can get the most out of the ECEEH modality.

How long do I need to send each individual symbol to myself or others?

Whenever you send energy, be it a symbol or simply a prayer or flow of light, there is theoretically no time limit on how long you can send the healing. Yet, you will intuitively know when it's time to stop. How? Because it's like riding a wave on the ocean of universal light. When you begin to send the energy, let's say you have your hands over the person's body, and you might not feel a thing at first. Then, all of a sudden, you feel a huge surge of flow coming from your hands. This may have a feeling of increase or becoming stronger with time. Then, next thing you know, that high octane surge slows down a bit, and soon it stops.

When I teach this to my gemstone students, I explain the fact that different stones have different frequencies, or waves of light, that comprise them. Remember in the first sections of the book when we talked about color frequencies and how they resonate with stones? Ruby, for example, is the red ray, and it is a lot slower frequency, or in other words, a longer wavelength, than let's say an amethyst the purple ray would be. Likewise, I believe people will take as much energy as they need for as long as they need it. They are filling up on something they need, kind of like when you go to the gas station to fill up your car. The longer it takes, the more fuel it needs, right? So, who's to say how long that will be? Typically, each flow of energy shouldn't take more than a few minutes each; but then again, if it does, it does.

When I worked with the test group on this modality, I could easily tell who liked which symbols best, or I should say who needed each symbol the most, based on the amount of time it took me to send each symbol to them. When it takes longer, then it means there's something the person needs to receive from that symbol. All this is to say, be open to allowing what happens to happen. There is no right or wrong. As long as you do your best and follow what you believe to be the truth for the person to whom you're sending the energy, then all is well.

When I use the symbols, do I have to give the descriptions of each as I use them? For example, if Hawk is Wisdom, do I need to send Wisdom with Hawk every time?

No. You certainly can allow the Hawk symbol to represent Wisdom and you can think of Wisdom as you send the symbol, but the symbol works, whether we think about the keynotes or not. Yes, I think it's good to envision the picture of the Hawk in your mind, and if you're sending energy, you may want to consciously send Wisdom to your client. That would be good, but it is not absolutely necessary. I've been working on some clients thinking of the image only when suddenly the word *Wisdom* pops in, and that's when I know the client needed that energy. I know it is helpful to think about the keynotes when visualizing your symbols, but the most important aspect of the healing session is to hold the intention that the person will use the Hawk symbol (for example) for whatever is for the highest and best. We don't always understand how a client will receive our healing or what the symbols will be used for specifically because theoretically that is none of our business. I say it that way because we are not in charge. We are channels for light. Nothing more. I don't want you to get so attached to the meanings and keynotes that you're not opening up to the Source of All That Is and allowing whatever is for the person's highest good to come through. So, the answer is yes, and no, and use your intuition.

Once I did this process a few times, I noticed that I don't seem to need all of the symbols as much as I used to. Is that right? If so, why not? What changed?

Great insight! The more you use these symbols and work with the ECEEH process, the more familiar they become to you on an energetic level. At some point, you might notice that you don't need all symbols all the time. One day a certain symbol might be super strong, then the next day you don't even use it at all. Just know that you are always guided and you will receive what you need. That is something which is determined by your own Higher Self and those of the clients you work on.

I asked you to initially bring each symbol down through your crown chakra because that way the energy has a chance to permeate your entire field, but for myself and my clients, the more we worked with the ECEEH modality, we soon realized that moving the symbols through the crown was no longer necessary. The symbols were already inegrated into our energy fields and had shifted the vibrations enough that they were not needed. You will know that happens when you try to send a symbol and don't sense a shift in energy. Or you felt a buzzing in the hands at first, but then that feeling went away. Additionally, you may have had an inner vision of what symbol to send, but now one symbol no longer shows up in your mind's eye. Once you experience things like this, that's a sure sign you received what you needed, a change was made on an energetic level, and you did not need that particular symbol as much, or at all, anymore.

Does that mean I won't ever need the symbol ever again?

No, not necessarily. The energy bodies, just like our physical selves are in flux all of the time. Because of that, you may find that the shift you created lasts awhile, but keep attempting to send each symbol anyway, because you never know when the symbol you didn't need starts showing up as helpful for you again in the future. Change is one of our only guarantees in this life, so be open and flexible and prepared for shifts on a daily basis.

I find this a lot with gemstones. You may be inexplicably drawn to a particular stone for quite awhile, then you want nothing to do with it anymore. That means you've started to resonate with the stone. It's made the necessary change in your field. Healing symbols are the same. Once the change succeeds, you won't need them.

General Comments about My Experiences

Now that we've answered, I hope, many of your questions, I'd like to give you some overall feedback about what I learned working with these symbols and the ECEEH modality.

When I first started working with Edgar Cayce's Egyptian Energy Healing, I really wanted to be able to align the seven symbols perfectly with our seven traditional chakra centers and simply do an overlay with a chart so it would be easy to say the Lamp opens the crown chakra, Beetle opens the third eye chakra, Cockerel opens the throat chakra, and so on, but between the Crown symbol which seems to work on our etheric field and the Serpent that shoots to the base of the spine like dormant Kundalini and will eventually move wherever it wants to, I don't believe such categorization of the ECEEH symbols is that simple. The energy is much more multidimensional than other systems I've worked with in the past.

I am also compelled to believe that this information is somehow energetically needed at this time and may be of assistance in future generations. Typically, when I work with energy healing, there is a sense of starting from a grounded place and moving the energy to a more expansive space of opening up to spirit and being much more in the etheric. In other words, when I first started doing my healing work, people needed to escape the daily grind and rise above the physical. That's not the case anymore. Our society, as a whole, is far less grounded than it used to be—to a point it's rather scary. People need to be brought back to earth to assist with what we're doing here, but instead, many people are connected to various devices and spend very little time in their bodies, to the detriment of all.

ECEEH starts out in the outer fields and dimensions of reality. The energy blasts you when you first receive it, and as you move through the seven symbols, there is a sense of bringing the spiritual bodies back to earth, and a real grounding feeling takes place that increases over time and gets stronger the more you practice. This is totally contrary to anything I have ever worked with before or have ever seen as a healer over the course of many years.

I believe this might be happening because our world is literally spinning out of control. As a society, we are becoming more fractured and isolated, and most people are in a collective trance, staring at their devices and allowing their minds to roam freely in space, into imaginary universes and spaces filled with fictional content rather than in a real waking reality. Escapism can be okay some of the time, if it helps alleviate stress; but when you have an entire species constantly floating out into the ethers, eventually a whole new set of problems and conditions emerges that simply did not exist before.

Sadly, our suicide rates are up, people are lonely and disconnected because the majority of the relationships we have these days are with cyber people whom we don't know and have never personally met.

Of course, I do believe there is hope. People are beginning to get together in groups to work on tasks; they are dancing and performing and eating together, which is good, but not everybody is participating. We are largely ungrounded, and I believe the ECEEH modality can assist us in grounding and shifting our frequencies to match the new energies coming to earth at this time. Using ECEEH expands our etheric fields and enables our physical bodies to be grounded and aligned on our planet at this time in history, which is a good thing.

Additionally, when I first began noticing the counterclockwise spinning that takes place at the end when the Lamp symbols are placed over the crown and feet to form the Way, I realized this motion is in rapport with the direction the earth spins. We are needed to become grounded and to get into better affinity with earth by literally spinning our energy centers, so we begin to align with our planet.

Years ago, when I first started teaching, I used the pendulum, which we discussed earlier in the book, to experiment with the directions our chakras were spinning at that time, and I noticed that men and women were different and that each chakra spun in opposite ways like gears on a wheel. I now feel all of us need to have our energy centers moving in the counterclockwise direction. In time, that could change, but for now, that's what needs to happen.

If you want to muscle test this, train your pendulum as I showed you and ask. I believe you will receive that same information. I am guided to instruct you on that at this time. If things change in the future, believe me, I'll let you know. I also mentioned *future generations* earlier, because cyclically, there might be a time when this information becomes irrelevant, yet years and years from now, perhaps someone will find at least some of the ECEEH regains its resonance again. All things come back in time, as they say.

These are my initial thoughts and I welcome hearing from you as you go on your own healing journey.

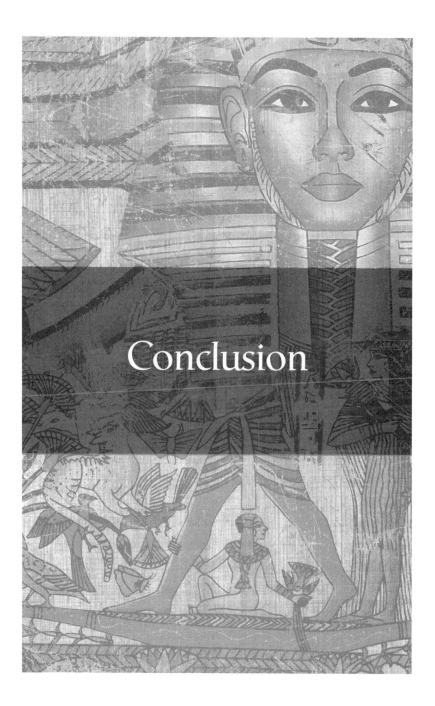

Conclusion

(Q) Is there any message concerning this period that would aid us in bringing love, harmony and peace, to those of the Egyptian period who are again to carry on this work?
(A) Just been given.   993-3

One thing I love about the Cayce readings is that Source did not mince words. Once a revelation was given, that was that. So, what answer had Cayce given previously to the heartfelt question about how to carry on with this healing mission?

> . . . Keep thine heart singing, for in thine own heart is BORN ANEW those blessings THOU may be to so many! Keep inviolate those words as HE points them OUT to thee, for "The way ye know," the faults ye know! BE patient, be kind, be gentle, with those who falter; for MANY lean upon thee!   993-3

Source's advice for our future conduct in relationship to others could not be timelier, especially in today's world. We need to do whatever we can to create greater camaraderie and fellowship with other sentient beings on our planet, and if tapping into Cayce's wisdom can assist us in taking a deep breath and connecting to the divine and to each other, then so be it.

I am left at the end of my long journey with this material once again feeling in a state of awe and wonderment. Every single time I open the life readings to begin one of these projects, I am completely blown away by the depth and the incredible range of topics Cayce blessed us with during his amazing life. I so hope that all who read this will find it valuable and that the material can be part of the Work that is carried on into the future so later generations may benefit.

I have learned a lot on this journey about Edgar Cayce, the life readings, and most importantly, about myself. I found discoveries in my research I had never seen before. I wonder how that could possibly happen, and yet with over 14,000 readings to pour through, I should have known I would find something new.

ECEEH is unlike any modality I have worked with thus far, and I can only attribute that to the ever-changing energies on our planet. As you move through the nine symbols, there is a sense of bringing the spiritual bodies back to earth, and the energy flow has a real grounding feeling that seems to increase in intensity over time. The vibrations become stronger and more pronounced the more you practice. I realize that it might take a while to know exactly how these energies are affecting our frequencies, and yet I do know, after using the symbols, that I feel a sense of clear peace and balance that has been quite helpful so far.

As Albert Einstein once said, "It will take a whole new way of thinking if humanity is to survive." Sadly, I think this is true, and I feel sure that this is how all of us former Atlanteans once felt during the destructions. Yet hope remains.

People are beginning to realize how technology has divided us and are now starting to come back together to share, to enjoy. That's a start. I just pray we can look up from our devices occasionally and into each other's eyes to connect on the heart and soul level.

Please let me know how you are doing with your healing practice. I'd love to hear from you. Above all, I hope this information has inspired you to explore the legacy of Edgar Cayce and to continue seeking as a Light Bearer and healer. I pray the information will be helpful now and in the future. Know I am sending you warm blessings on your path, now and always. Namaste!

Bibliography

Books

Andrews, Shirley. *Atlantis: Insights from a Lost Civilization.* St. Paul, MN: Llewellyn Publications, 1997.

Andrews, Ted. *Animal Speak: The Spiritual & Magical Powers of Creatures Great and Small.* St. Paul, MN: Llewellyn Publications, 1993.

———. *How to Heal with Color.* St. Paul, MN: Llewellyn Publications, 1993.

———. *How to See and Read the Aura.* St. Paul, MN: Llewellyn Publications, 2001.

Budge, E.A. Wallis. *An Egyptian Hieroglyphic Dictionary Volume One.* New York, NY: Dover Publications, Inc., 1978.

Chopra, Deepak. *Quantum Healing: Exploring the Frontiers of Mind/Body Medicine.* New York, NY: Bantam Books, 1989.

———. *The Seven Spiritual Laws of Success.* San Rafael, CA: New World Library Amber-Allen Publishing, 1993.

Cooper, J.D. *An Illustrated Encyclopaedia of Traditional Symbols.* London: Thames & Hudson Ltd., 1978.

Cotterell, Maurice. *The Tutankhamen Prophecies: The Sacred Secret of the Maya, Egyptians and Freemasons.* Rochester, VT: Bear & Company, 2001.

Cunningham, Scott. *Earth Air Fire and Water.* St. Paul, MN: Llewellyn Publications, 1991.

Doreal. *The Emerald Tablets of Thoth-The Atlantean.* Sedalia, CO: Brotherhood of the White Temple, Inc. 1992.

Drury, Nevill. *Shamanism: An Introductory Guide to Living in Harmony with Nature.* Boston, MA: Element Books, 2000.

Gerber, Richard. *Vibrational Healing.* Santa Fe, NM: Bear & Company, 1988.

Hay, Louise L. *Heal Your Body: The Mental Causes for Physical Illness and the Metaphysical Way to Overcome Them.* Carlsbad, CA: Hay House, Inc., 1982.

Kaehr, Shelley, PhD. *Edgar Cayce's Guide to Gemstones, Minerals, Metals & More.* Virginia Beach, VA: A.R.E. Press, 2005.

———. *Edgar Cayce's Sacred Stones.* Virginia Beach, VA: A.R.E. Press, 2015.

———. *Holographic Mapping: Energy Healing Made Simple.* Dallas, TX: Out of

This World Publishing, 2014.

———. *Supretrovie: Externally Induced Past Life Memories.* Dallas, TX: Out of This World Publishing, 2016.

Schiegl, Heinz. *Healing Magnetism.* York Beach, Maine: Samuel Weiser, Inc., 1987.

Sharamon, Shalila, and Bodo J. Baginski. *The Chakra Handbook.* Wilmot, WI: Lotus Light Publications, 1991.

Sherwood, Keith. *Chakra Therapy.* St. Paul, MN: Llewellyn Publications, 1988.

Stein, Diane. *Essential Reiki.* Freedom, CA: The Crossing Press, Inc., 1995.

Stone, Robert B., PhD. *The Secret Life of Your Cells.* Atglen, PA: Whitford Press, 1989.

Todeschi, Kevin. *Edgar Cayce on Vibrations: Spirits in Motion.* Virginia Beach, VA: A.R.E. Press, 2007.

———, and Carol Ann Liaros. *Edgar Cayce on Auras and Colors.* Virginia Beach, VA: A.R.E. Press, 2011.

Van Auken, John. *Edgar Cayce on Health, Healing & Rejuvenation.* Virginia Beach, VA: A.R.E. Press, 2016.

Virtue, Doreen. *Healing with the Angels: How the Angels Can Assist You in Every Area of Your Life.* Carlsbad, CA: Hay House, 1999.

Wright, Machaelle Small. *MAP: The Co-Creative White Brotherhood Medical Assistance Program.* Warrenton, VA: Perelandra, Ltd., 1990.

Articles (Print and Web) and Documentaries

Demers, Dawn. "The 7 Archangels and Their Meanings: Connect to the archangel that specializes in the area of your life that you wish to improve." http://www.beliefnet.com/inspiration/angels/galleries/the-7-archangels-and-their-meanings.aspx?

"Essential Oils in the Ancient World, pt. I," April 13, 2015, https://www.youngliving.com/blog/essential-oils-in-the-ancient-world-pt-i/

Goldsmith, Jo. "An Investigation into the Relationship Between Sound and Color," http://www.people.vcu.edu/~djbromle/color-theory/color01/Relationship-color-sound-joe_goldsmith.html

"How Old Are the Pyramids?" *Nova Online Adventure*, 1997, http://www.pbs.org/wgbh/nova/pyramid/explore/howold.html

Kaehr, Shelley, PhD. "Cayce on Art & Emotions: Attuning to the Infinite," *Venture Inward Magazine*, Winter 2018, p.18–20.

Leech, Joe, M.S. "10 Evidence Based Benefits of Cinnamon." *Healthonline.com*, https://www.healthline.com/nutrition/10-proven-benefits-of-cinnamon

Mark, Joshua J. "Festivals in Ancient Egypt," *Ancient History Encyclopedia*, March 17, 2017, Web. 12 June 2018, https://www.ancient.eu/article/1032/festivals-in-ancient-egypt/

Mosley, Michael. "The Second Brain in Our Stomachs," *BBC TV*, July 11, 2012, https://www.bbc.com/news/health-18779997

Ouellette, Jennifer. "40 People Got Burned 'Firewalking' in Texas for the Dumbest Reason," Gizmodo.com, 6/24/16, 12:35pm, https://gizmodo.com/40-people-got-burned-firewalking-in-texas-for-the-dumbe-1782559421

Sovik, Rolf, and Dick Ravizza. "Self Study: Nostril Dominance," *Yoga International*, https://yogainternational.com/article/view/self-study-nostril-dominance

Taylor, Ashley P. "Newton's Color Theory, ca. 1665 Newton's rainbow forms the familiar ROYGBIV because he thought the range of visible colors should be analogous to the seven-note musical scale," *The Scientist*, March 1, 2017, https://www.the-scientist.com/foundations/newtons-color-theory-ca-1665-31931

Whitman, Sarah. "Differences in Hawks and Falcons," Pets on mom.me, https://animals.mom.me/differences-hawks-falcons-8511.html

Website Resources List

The following list will provide more information and further reading about some of the topics discussed in the book. Enjoy!

Affirmation. http://www.dictionary.com/browse/affirmation?s=t

Ancient Egyptian Soul. https://en.wikipedia.org/wiki/Ancient_Egyptian_concept_of_the_soul

Animism. https://en.wikipedia.org/wiki/Animism

Ankh. https://en.wikipedia.org/wiki/Ankh

Book of Enoch. https://en.wikipedia.org/wiki/Book_of_Enoch

Cedar Oil. https://en.wikipedia.org/wiki/Cedar_oil

Chakra. https://en.wikipedia.org/wiki/Chakra

Cinnamon. https://en.wikipedia.org/wiki/Cinnamon

Crowns of Egypt. https://en.wikipedia.org/wiki/Crowns_of_Egypt

Deshret. https://en.wikipedia.org/wiki/Deshret

Earth's Rotation. https://en.wikipedia.org/wiki/Earth%27s_rotation

Emoji. http://www.dictionary.com/browse/emoji?s=t

Firewalking. https://en.wikipedia.org/wiki/Firewalking

Gate Deities of the Underworld. https://en.wikipedia.org/wiki/Gate_deities_of_the_underworld

Hedjet. https://en.wikipedia.org/wiki/Hedjet

Horus. https://en.wikipedia.org/wiki/Horus

Isaac Newton. https://en.wikipedia.org/wiki/Isaac_Newton

Juniper. https://www.webmd.com/vitamins/ai/ingredientmono-724/juniper

Khepri. https://en.wikipedia.org/wiki/Khepri

Kyphi. https://en.wikipedia.org/wiki/Kyphi

Lethe. https://en.wikipedia.org/wiki/Lethe

Magnesium Sulfate. https://en.wikipedia.org/wiki/Magnesium_sulfate

Myrrh. https://en.wikipedia.org/wiki/Myrrh

Opticks. https://en.wikipedia.org/wiki/Opticks

Pschent. https://en.wikipedia.org/wiki/Pschent

Reiki. https://en.wikipedia.org/wiki/Reiki

Rooster. https://en.wikipedia.org/wiki/Rooster

Sage. https://www.webmd.com/vitamins/ai/ingredientmono-504/sage

Scarab (Artifact). https://en.wikipedia.org/wiki/Scarab_(artifact)

Scarabaeus Sacer. https://en.wikipedia.org/wiki/Scarabaeus_sacer

Serpent. https://en.wikipedia.org/wiki/Serpent_(symbolism)

Supretrovie. https://www.amazon.com/s?k=supretrovie&ref=nb_sb_noss

Table Salt. https://en.wikipedia.org/wiki/Salt

Thoth. https://en.wikipedia.org/wiki/Thoth

Upanishads. https://en.wikipedia.org/wiki/Upanishads

Usui, Mikao. https://en.wikipedia.org/wiki/Mikao_Usui

Vedas. https://en.wikipedia.org/wiki/Vedas

Violet Flame. https://www.summitlighthouse.org/violet-flame/

Wadjet. https://en.wikipedia.org/wiki/Wadjet

White Brotherhood. https://www.summitlighthouse.org/great-white-brotherhood/

About the Author

Shelley Kaehr, PhD is one of the world's leading authorities on energy healing and mind–body medicine and the author of numerous books, including *Edgar Cayce's Guide to Gemstones, Minerals, Metals & More* and *Edgar Cayce's Sacred Stones*, both published by the A.R.E. Press.

A world traveler and popular guest speaker, Dr. Kaehr is a leading expert on the practical use of gems and minerals to shift energetic patterns and frequencies. She has trained thousands of energy healing practitioners during her many years in private practice and has developed healing modalities such as Holographic Mapping before developing the Edgar Cayce's Egyptian Energy Healing method.

A world-renowned past-life regressionist, Dr. Shelley's method has been endorsed by numerous leaders in the field of consciousness, including Dr. Brian Weiss who called her book *Lifestream*, "An important contribution to the field of regression therapy." She believes our memories are stored holographically in the energetic fields around our bodies, and by combining hypnosis with energy healing, lasting change is achieved.

Shelley would love to hear from readers about their experiences with Edgar Cayce's Egyptian Energy Healing. Write her at shelley@shelleykaehr.com or send her a text to (214)699-8611.

Connect with Dr. Shelley online:
https://pastlifelady.com
Join the discussion on her Facebook Fan Page: Past Life Lady
Follow her on Instagram: shelleykaehr
You Tube Channel: Past Life Lady
Twitter: @ShelleyKaehr

Reference Page
for the
ECEEH Symbols

Lamp of the Light
Bearers = Illumination

Hawk
= Wisdom

Beetle = World

Cross = Life

Crown = Power

Cockerel = Birth

Gate/Door
= Ascension

Serpent = Mind

Way
= Source

A.R.E. PRESS

Edgar Cayce (1877–1945) founded the non-profit Association for Research and Enlightenment (A.R.E.) in 1931, to explore spirituality, holistic health, intuition, dream interpretation, psychic development, reincarnation, and ancient mysteries—all subjects that frequently came up in the more than 14,000 documented psychic readings given by Cayce.

Edgar Cayce's A.R.E. provides individuals from all walks of life and a variety of religious backgrounds with tools for personal transformation and healing at all levels—body, mind, and spirit.

A.R.E. Press has been publishing since 1931 as well, with the mission of furthering the work of A.R.E. by publishing books, DVDs, and CDs to support the organization's goal of helping people to change their lives for the better physically, mentally, and spiritually.

In 2009, A.R.E. Press launched its second imprint, 4th Dimension Press. While A.R.E. Press features topics directly related to the work of Edgar Cayce and often includes excerpts from the Cayce readings, 4th Dimension Press allows us to take our publishing efforts further with like-minded and expansive explorations into the mysteries and spirituality of our existence without direct reference to Cayce specific content.

A.R.E. Press/4th Dimension Press
215 67th Street
Virginia Beach, VA 23451

Learn more at EdgarCayce.org. Visit ARECatalog.com to browse and purchase additional titles.

ARE PRESS.COM

Who Was Edgar Cayce?
Twentieth Century Psychic and Medical Clairvoyant

Edgar Cayce (pronounced Kay-Cee, 1877-1945) has been called the "sleeping prophet," the "father of holistic medicine," and the most-documented psychic of the 20th century. For more than 40 years of his adult life, Cayce gave psychic "readings" to thousands of seekers while in an unconscious state, diagnosing illnesses and revealing lives lived in the past and prophecies yet to come. But who, exactly, was Edgar Cayce?

Cayce was born on a farm in Hopkinsville, Kentucky, in 1877, and his psychic abilities began to appear as early as his childhood. He was able to see and talk to his late grandfather's spirit, and often played with "imaginary friends" whom he said were spirits on the other side. He also displayed an uncanny ability to memorize the pages of a book simply by sleeping on it. These gifts labeled the young Cayce as strange, but all Cayce really wanted was to help others, especially children.

Later in life, Cayce would find that he had the ability to put himself into a sleep-like state by lying down on a couch, closing his eyes, and folding his hands over his stomach. In this state of relaxation and meditation, he was able to place his mind in contact with all time and space—the universal consciousness, also known as the super-conscious mind. From there, he could respond to questions as broad as, "What are the secrets of the universe?" and "What is my purpose in life?" to as specific as, "What can I do to help my arthritis?" and "How were the pyramids of Egypt built?" His responses to these questions came to be called "readings," and their insights offer practical help and advice to individuals even today.

The majority of Edgar Cayce's readings deal with holistic health and the treatment of illness. Yet, although best known for this material, the sleeping Cayce did not seem to be limited to concerns about the physical body. In fact, in their entirety, the readings discuss an astonishing 10,000 different topics. This vast array of subject matter can be narrowed down into a smaller group of topics that, when compiled together, deal with the following five categories: (1) Health-Related Information; (2) Philosophy and Reincarnation; (3) Dreams and Dream Interpretation; (4) ESP and Psychic Phenomena; and (5) Spiritual Growth, Meditation, and Prayer.

Learn more at EdgarCayce.org.

What Is A.R.E.?

Edgar Cayce founded the non-profit Association for Research and Enlightenment (A.R.E.) in 1931, to explore spirituality, holistic health, intuition, dream interpretation, psychic development, reincarnation, and ancient mysteries—all subjects that frequently came up in the more than 14,000 documented psychic readings given by Cayce.

The Mission of the A.R.E. is to help people transform their lives for the better, through research, education, and application of core concepts found in the Edgar Cayce readings and kindred materials that seek to manifest the love of God and all people and promote the purposefulness of life, the oneness of God, the spiritual nature of humankind, and the connection of body, mind, and spirit.

With an international headquarters in Virginia Beach, Va., a regional headquarters in Houston, regional representatives throughout the U.S., Edgar Cayce Centers in more than thirty countries, and individual members in more than seventy countries, the A.R.E. community is a global network of individuals.

A.R.E. conferences, international tours, camps for children and adults, regional activities, and study groups allow like-minded people to gather for educational and fellowship opportunities worldwide.

A.R.E. offers membership benefits and services that include a quarterly body-mind-spirit member magazine, Venture Inward, a member newsletter covering the major topics of the readings, and access to the entire set of readings in an exclusive online database.

Learn more at EdgarCayce.org.

EDGARCAYCE.ORG